MASTERING

DIRECT ACCESS

FUNDAMENTALS

MASTERING DIRECT ACCESS FUNDAMENTALS

Understanding Market Information and Learning the Key Skills to Become a Successful Electronic Trader

Jonathan Aspatore
with Dan Bress

McGraw-Hill
New York   Chicago   San Francisco
Lisbon   London   Madrid   Mexico City   Milan
New Delhi   San Juan   Seoul   Singapore
Sydney   Toronto

Library of Congress Cataloging-in-Publication Data

Aspatore, Jonathan Reed.
    Mastering direct access fundamentals :   understanding market information and learning the key skills to become a successful electronic trader / by Jonathan R. Aspatore with Dan Bress.
        p.   cm.
    ISBN 0-07-136249-5
    I. Electronic trading of securities.   I. Bress, Dan.   II. Title.

HG4515.95 .A849 2000
332.63'2'02854678—dc21

00–053700

McGraw-Hill

*A Division of The **McGraw·Hill** Companies*

The sponsoring editor for this book was Stephen Isaacs, the editing supervisor was Ruth W. Mannino, and the production supervisor was Charles Annis.

Printed and bound by Quebecor/Martinsburg.

This publication is designed to provide accurate and authoritative information in regard to the subject matter covered. It is sold with the understanding that neither the author nor the publisher is engaged in rendering legal, accounting, or other professional service. If legal advice or other expert assistance is required, the services of a competent professional person should be sought.
—*From a Declaration of Principles jointly adopted by a Committee of the American Bar Association and a Committee of Publishers*

The viewpoints and content expressed by the authors are their own and not those of Tradescape.com, Inc. or any of its affiliated entities, employees, officers, directors, or authorized representatives (the "Company"). The Company does not endorse any of the content contained herein and has not verified the accuracy of any of the content. The information is not to be construed as investment advice, and any reliance on the content as contained herein is at the reader's sole risk and liability.

Tradescape1.0™ and TradescapePro™ are trademarks of Tradescape.com, Inc.; NexTrade™, of NexTrade Holdings, Inc., Raging Bull™, of Lycos, Inc., and Ameritrade™, of Ameritrade, Inc.; Island® is a registered trademark of The Island ECN, Inc., Briefing.com®, of Briefing.com, Inc., Silicon Investor®, of InfoSpace, Inc., Attain®, of All-Tech Direct, Inc., and E*TRADE®, of E*TRADE, Inc. All other trademarked products mentioned are used in an editorial fashion only, and to the benefit of the trademark owner, with no intention of infringement of the trademark. Where such designations appear in this book, they have been printed with initial caps.

CONTENTS

PREFACE

Mastering Direct Access Trading is part of the six-book series on direct access trading from McGraw-Hill. The series of books represents the first detailed look at every element of direct access trading for individuals interested in harnessing the amazing changes occurring in the world's financial markets. All the books contain a clear and basic approach on how to take advantage of direct access to the markets for your specific level of investing/trading. Direct access trading is for everyone, and in this series of books, we show you how to take advantage of it if you only place a couple of trades a year, if you are starting to get more active in the markets, or even if you want to be a day trader. Take advantage of these revolutionary changes today, and start accessing the markets directly with direct access trading. Good luck!

ACKNOWLEDGMENTS

A special thanks to everyone at Tradescape and McGraw-Hill for their help in writing this groundbreaking series of books, especially Sohail Khalid, Alison Friedman, Michelle Hifai, and Stephen Isaacs.

1

WHAT THIS BOOK WILL DO FOR YOU

This book is meant to help you master the fundamentals of direct access trading. Whether you aspire to become a full-time day trader, a part-time day trader, or simply use direct access trading for your longer-term investments, we will help you master the basics so that you can take advantage of the revolutionary new technologies changing the world's financial markets. The technology behind direct access trading will some day be used by the majority of the world's traders and inves-tors. It enables individuals to do things never before possible and trade with the same tools as the Wall Street professionals. Although the abun-dance of new information you are introduced to may seem over-whelming at first, over time you will learn to weed out the information that is of no use and focus only on specific pieces that are. If you have bought this book, it means that you are already ahead of the learning curve with respect to the rest of the world. As the world's financial

1

markets all become more "direct" in nature, individuals who have mastered direct access fundamentals will be well positioned to capitalize on the "low-hanging fruit" that evolves over time. Spend as much time as you can to get as much as possible out of this book by researching interesting topics on the Internet, using simulation devices at various direct access trading Web sites, and filling out the worksheets at the end of this book.

This book will discuss trading expectations, developing a trading strategy, basic analysis, interpreting real-time news and indicators, and trading for a living. Each chapter contains information for every type of direct access trader. Remember that even though you may fall squarely into being a day trader, part-time day trader, or long-term direct access trader, it helps to understand the mindset of each. Therefore, you can adjust your strategy over time and take advantage of direct access trading on multiple levels. Direct access trading is for everyone on some level.

The best way to get comfortable with direct access trading is to start small. Therefore, by providing information throughout the book on all different levels of traders, both short and long term, it helps people get started and find out if they want to devote more time and resources to it, and vice versa. Direct access trading is not difficult if you have the right expectations and devote the proper amount of time to it. This book contains the following information for aspiring new day traders, part-time day traders, and long-term direct access traders:

Day traders. Becoming a successful day trader is not something that happens overnight. Over the course of the following chapters, this book will show you the best ways to "ease" into day trading. This book will show you how to test your skills and make sure you are cut out for the world of day trading. The people who have the most success with day trading are the ones who spend the appropriate amount of time learning the fundamentals of day trading and then applying them in the markets only after weeks or months of training. Although it takes a different amount of time for each individual, depending on his or her background and learning environment, every day trader needs to master the fundamentals discussed in this book. For example, one of the most important skills for a day trader is to be quick on the keyboard. Day traders must be able to quickly enter and exit positions, pull up news, and perform other tasks in a matter of seconds—and *without* looking down at their fingers. Regardless of whether or not you are a great typist, it takes time to learn the new keystrokes and memorize what they mean. Remember, one or two wrong keystrokes can mean a whole lot of trouble. Keyboard basics is just one example of the fundamentals that day traders must master. The following chapters also will help you set expectations, develop your trading strategy, identify which stocks to trade, understand basic analysis to use in the markets, and interpret real-time indicators.

Part-time day traders. Becoming a part-time day trader means that you have to learn the basics of both day trading and long-term direct access trading. However, in the long run, you will be well served by understanding these two very different trading styles. In fact, some of the most successful traders in the world employ both styles to maximize and preserve their investment capital. How do you do both, you might ask? Well, part-time day traders need to focus on a much smaller segment of the market than full-time day traders because they are not devoting as much time to it. However, just because they are not full-time day traders does not means they can ignore the market for days at a stretch. They need to pick one to three stocks and get to know them day in and day out. Alternatively, some part-time day traders only focus on stocks that are having an initial public offering, partly because they often have the biggest "pop" and partly because traditionally they cannot get shares until the stock has "popped" using their traditional online investing firm. Part-time day traders then need to allocate part of their overall investment capital for day trading. It should only be an amount with which they are comfortable withstanding huge swings—and ultimately potentially losing as well. A lot of individuals use part-time day trading to test their skills to see if they could make it as a full-time day trader. This is an excellent idea, but you must realize that you still need to spend a significant amount of time honing your skills before you enter the live day trading arena. Just because you are now comfortable using direct access trading tools for your longer-term investments does not mean that you are ready to jump into the day trading world. This book will help you take the appropriate steps to find out if part-time day trading is something that interests you, and will provide you with ways to use day trading as a building block to potentially become a full-time day trader.

The following chapters also will help you set expectations, develop your trading strategy, identify which stocks to trade, understand basic analysis to use in the markets, and interpret real-time indicators.

Long-term direct access traders. At some point in the future every investor will be a direct access trader. However, because the technology is only now being used by early adopters, we call individuals who are using direct access trading tools for their longer-term investments *long-term direct access traders.* Although this name eventually will become obsolete, and everyone will be "trading" or "investing," however you want to put it, in the same manner, for now we shall use this term. Mastering the fundamentals of direct access trading can be intimidating at first depending on your previous exposure to the markets, but do not be overwhelmed. This book highlights the fundamentals that will help you become 100 percent comfortable using this revolutionary new technology. Remember, everyone eventually will have to learn how to use the technology in some fashion or another, and those who are in from the beginning stand to capitalize the most. Everyone asks direct access traders, "What about the professionals out there just waiting to eat you alive?" Remember, however, that these professionals have always been out there. Even when you invested through a third party such as a broker, they were out there. You just now have the tools to compete with them on even ground. In the past, it was like you had one hand tied behind your back. In addition, because you are not looking at making intraday trades, you are simply using better tools and technology to make investments—how is there a greater risk in this? Although the interface for direct access trading is not yet as "user-friendly" as traditional online brokerages, mastering fundamentals such as the keyboard should not be a prohibiting step. Enjoy the fact that you are an early adopter of this new medium. Correct other people if they call you a day trader and explain to them how you are using this technology to get better information and prices for your long-term investments. Eventually, they will see the light, and we will all trade this way. The following chapters also will help you set expectations, develop your trading strategy, identify which stocks to trade, understand basic analysis to use in the markets, and interpret real-time indicators.

WORKSHEETS

At the end of this book we also present you with a series of worksheets to help get you started. By spending the proper amount of time doing these worksheets, you will force yourself to answer questions that will make your direct access trading experience much more profitable. Direct access trading is for everyone—it just depends on what level. These worksheets will help you "get your house in order" before you make the jump to becoming a direct access trader. They are on topics such as risk profiles, trader type analysis, financial goals, and other issues of importance for every direct access trader.

AND FINALLY

After reading this book, you should have a clear understanding of what you need to do to master the fundamentals of direct access trading. Depending on your background and direct access trading aspirations, the result clearly will be different for everyone. However, there are certain key fundamentals that you must master if you are to use direct access trading tools at all. In addition, there are probably things you may have never thought of that are critical to direct access trading, such as mastering the keyboard. Direct access trading is different from any other type of online investing or after-hours trading, but regardless of your experience with either, this book will help point you in the right direction for where you should be spending your time learning. And most important, you will be ahead of the curve in terms of understanding how to capitalize on where the world's financial markets are heading.

It is also important to understand that this book should just be your first step in getting started in direct access trading. We do not recommend that anyone goes out and opens a "live" account before spending a considerable amount of time planning a strategy, establishing a risk-reward profile, and using simulation tools. And if you want to engage in day trading at any level, make sure you only use money that you can realistically afford to lose. Direct access trading presents an incredibly powerful set of tools into the hands of every individual who uses them. The key is to make sure that you clearly outline your intentions before just jumping in. Congratulations on making your first step into the world of direct access trading. Make sure to also look at the other books in this series, including *Understanding Direct Access Trading, Tools for the Direct Access Trader, Direct Access Execution, Technical Analysis for Direct Access Trading,* and *Trading Strategies for Direct Access Trading.* Take advantage of this empowering new technology for investors and traders of all levels today!

2

EXPECTATIONS

Having the right level of expectations for every level of direct access trading is a must. Individuals who get into direct access trading expecting to become instant millionaires are going to be in deep trouble— usually very quickly—because they make huge trades without the proper level of experience. However, individuals who have realistic expectations and give themselves the proper time and training to become familiar with their new tools will profit in the long run. Just like learning anything new, direct access trading takes time to learn.

Direct access trading should be taken very seriously. Direct access trading carries the same risks as any type of investing. Although there are a plethora of stories about the "nouveau riche" of the direct access trading world, only those who take it very seriously have such a high degree of success. The key is to approach direct access trading with your eyes wide open. However, just because now you have available to you the same tools as Wall Street professionals, there is no guarantee of success. Direct access trading can be as conservative or as risky as you want to make it. Your trading strategy and goals should be realistic from the beginning. A good trading strategy coupled with unbridled discipline ultimately is the best recipe for success.

WHAT SHOULD I EXPECT?

Just because you may be an expert investor does not mean that you can automatically just switch over to direct access trading and become an expert overnight. On the other hand, even if you are completely new to online investing, you can still easily make the jump to direct access trading with the proper education and guidance. Although it definitely helps to have some level of investing experience, the same lessons you learn from direct access trading apply to any type of trading. Therefore, regardless of your previous level of financial or trading expertise, you are going to need to spend some time learning about how to really capitalize on direct access trading. A lot of new direct access traders are amazed at the wealth of new information available to them. Although it may seem overwhelming at first, realize that every direct access trader only uses pieces of this information. Each individual customizes his or her screen in order to have exactly the pieces of news and information he or she needs to place trades. Everyone needs to spend some time getting comfortable with the new tools, accessing to real-time information, and understanding how to interpret pieces of information that never before were available. Therefore, in the short run, expect that it will not be easy, but in the long run, it will be an extremely worthwhile and hopefully profitable experience.

HOW MUCH CAN I REALLY MAKE?

Direct access traders are like every other person who invests in stocks. Depending on how much risk they take on in the marketplace, they can expect their profits or losses to adjust accordingly. Some of the world's best day traders make millions of dollars every year, whereas others who are part-time direct access traders simply make an extra $25,000 to $50,000 every year. And other long-term direct access traders simply use the tools to save a couple of hundred dollars on every trade by getting in at the best price possible. Nevertheless, how much you make really depends on your trading strategy and how much risk you take on in the marketplace. It also depends on how much money you have to trade with. Every trader works to steadily build a capital base, and as it grows, it becomes easier to make (or lose) larger amounts. By having a conservative trading strategy, you have a much better chance of growing your capital base steadily over time. However, every individual has a different trading strategy, and some of the best direct access traders have made their names accumulating large positions in the marketplace. The key is just to make sure that whatever you are doing coincides with your trading strategy and that you are comfortable with the risk.

The key for every direct access trader is to be realistic. Do not expect to come in and make a killing as a day trader in your first month. Also, do not expect to be able to even make a long-term trade with direct access trading tools without any education or practice. There is no hard and fast rule with respect to how long it takes to master the fundamentals of direct access trading. Each person can expect to spend some time on a simulator before placing any short- or long-term trades so that he or she comprehends the look and feel of direct access trading. Do not expect to be able to day trade just because you have faired well with your investments in the past. Direct access trading takes time for everyone to learn. In the long run, through the use of direct access trading tools you should be able to significantly improve your chances for getting in and out of stocks at the best prices possible and improving your overall profit potential. In addition, as other direct access trading opportunities become more prominent, such as New York Stock Exchange (NYSE) stocks and international stocks, you shall be well situated to be an early participant in capitalizing on these opportunities. In the long run, individuals who use direct access trading tools will have a definite edge over other online investors and people using third-party brokers. Your investment of time now will be well worth it over the long run.

WHAT HAPPENS IF THE MARKET CRASHES?

There has been a lot of discussion regarding what will happen to everyone if the market crashes. The only honest answer anyone can give you is that they simply do not know. There are hundreds of speculative ideas with respect to market crashes, but the only thing that holds true every time is that the market reacts differently every time. Whenever there is a bull market for an extended period of time, individuals always emerge who throw "doomsday" thoughts out into the mix. Conversely, whenever there is a bear market for an extended period of time, there are usually even more individuals who predict that an upturn in the markets is just around the corner. The bottom line for direct access traders is that all of this is really secondary. Regardless of the state of the markets, you will be better positioned than ever to capitalize on the upswings and get out of your positions if the market starts to tank. The reason for this is that direct access traders simply have better tools than traditional online investors or other individuals using a broker. Although it may be a little harder at first to learn how to use these tools, there is no additional risk if you are using direct access trading tools to perform the same functions as you were before. Let us look at a couple scenarios to show you the different effects on various types of direct access traders.

Day traders. Most members of the financial community has convinced themselves that the only reason that day traders are flourishing is because of the bull market. This is partly true, but trading in some form or another has always existed in our society—and has always been profitable. The only difference is that now individuals are doing the same things that other people at the venerable big name Wall Street firms are doing—and keeping the profits for themselves. Undeniably, day traders flourish more in bull markets, but day traders are just like any other traders. They short stocks as well and make money on them when they go down. In fact, many day traders claim that their favorite type of day is one in which there was a significant downturn in the markets the day before. They claim that this often creates a sort of "yard sale" mentality when normal investors are exiting their positions at low prices, driving prices even lower, and creating great buying opportunities for those with the capital to deploy. Every day trader is different, but most of them go long on the majority of their trades. This is so because their risk potential becomes more magnified when they short a stock; because a stock can run up to infinity but only down to zero, most day traders predominantly buy stocks in the hope that they will go up. If the market were to crash, day traders actually would be some of the best-positioned individuals. This is so because they would be able to get their money out of the market the quickest (because they are following the markets so closely every day while others are at their jobs doing something else) and then have the capital to deploy on stocks they feel got unjustly hit the hardest once the crash ends. A prolonged market correction, however, would have a significant effect on many day traders, especially if they keep going long on stocks in anticipation that they are going to turn around and the stocks just keep going lower day after day. A thing to do when there is a crash or market correction is to adjust your risk profile. By doing so, you can make sure that you are not too overexposed in the market and ready to jump back in once you are more comfortable with the market conditions.

Part-time day traders. Part-time day traders probably have the greatest amount of risk if the market crashes. This is so simply because they may be tempted to "overplay" the market by cashing out of their long-term positions and trying to day trade stocks they feel are at a bargain. The key for part-time day traders is to stick to their trading strategy. Just because the market is crashing or in a correction, you still need to stay disciplined. If you sense opportunity to day trade the couple of stocks that you are monitoring, it can be a great buying opportunity. However, understand that when the market in general is in a significant downturn, stocks tend to act differently. Therefore, it is important to adapt your risk parameters so that you are not overexposed in the market. In addition, because during a crash the market is prone to move very rapidly, it may be a good idea not to day trade at all during this time unless you can really spend the appropriate time monitoring your positions. When the market is in such a volatile state, it is possible for the market as a whole to be down a couple of hundred points in the morning, up a couple of hundred points in the afternoon, and then back down a couple of hundred points in the last hour of trading before the close. With this sort of volatility, you really need to be monitoring your intraday positions constantly, and unless you are extremely experienced, these are the sorts of days you should either day trade the whole day or not at all. For your longer-term investments, do not be tempted to exit them if your investment strategy is to hold onto them long term. Stocks go up and down over the course of every year, and market studies show that even with the crashes in the markets over the last 20 years, stocks have always bounced back. However, if you are confident that the stock is unjustly being lowered because of the overall market conditions and are comfortable with the risk that your position may go up, then it may be a good time to sell until the market cools down. As a part-time day trader, however, you need to keep the lines very defined between the stocks you day trade and your longer-term positions. Do not be tempted to pay too much attention to your longer-term positions and effectively end up day trading them if they really are long-term positions. For most part-time day traders, it is usually a good idea to leave longer-term positions alone unless you had previously indicated a particular strategy if the stock hit such a level.

Long-term direct access traders. Long-term traders who are using direct access trading tools for their normal investments will not be affected any differently if the market crashes than if they were still trading through a third party. In fact, should they decide they want to exit some of their positions before they go down too far, they will have the tools to exit them more quickly than they ever could have before. The key for them is not to overplay their stocks. It can be very tempting with the power of direct access trading tools to try to get in and out of your positions more often than you normally would. The key is not to do this unless there is an extraordinary situation that warrants such measures. Even this should not happen more than a couple of times a year. If you are a true long-term investor using these tools, over time stocks have proven to rise even with market crashes and corrections. However, if you keep on top of market conditions and feel that there is going to be a significant event that will drastically reduce the value of one or more of your stocks, then do not be afraid to put your money into cash until you feel the tide has turned. No longer do you have to sit on the sideline and wait for your broker to call you back or sit idly at your computer screen waiting for a confirmation and seeing what price you were able to exit at. If such a situation warrants, you can now exit these positions on your own terms and timetable.

HOW HARD IS THIS REALLY TO LEARN?

Mastering direct access trading fundamentals is not an impossible task, but it does require a commitment to learn and realistic expectations about what you can achieve. Just like learning anything else new, it takes time to learn some of the basics. Some people may ask why they should learn this if they can just sit at home and use their traditional online investing accounts. Well, the bad thing for these individuals is that they could miss out on some great investment opportunities by not being an "early adopter" of these new tools. Over time, most individuals will be using direct access trading tools, whether they know it or not. However, because we are in the early stages of this new phenomenon, most of the world is still unaware that it even exists. Learning how to use direct access trading tools is not that different from learning how to do any other new thing. In fact, what you are using it to do—invest in stocks—you probably already have some level of experience with. Therefore, what you are really learning how to do is to master the new set of tools available to you and capitalize on their functionality in ways never before possible. For some people, it can take months to learn how to use these tools; for others, it can take a matter of weeks. It really depends on the extent to which you plan on using the tools. Later in this book we talk a little about the specific time requirements and what you can expect when you first get started.

MISCONCEPTIONS

There are a ton of misconceptions regarding direct access trading tools. Because most of the members of the press initially surrounded day traders who were using these tools, direct access trading started off getting a somewhat tainted name. What the general public did not realize was that the technology day traders were using would become the foundation for the way all of us would trade in only a matter of years. In fact, even some of the major online brokerage firms are already starting to enable online investors to trade after hours on electronic communication networks (ECNs). Direct access trading tools eventually will revolutionize the way every trade is made worldwide. Look already at the differences between the NYSE and the Nasdaq. The computerized nature of the Nasdaq has vaulted the exchange to the forefront of our markets. In fact, as of right now, almost 99 percent of the direct access trades made are for Nasdaq stocks. Although this will change over time as the NYSE gets more "computerized," it is still a significant indicator of changing times. Thus, how hard is it to learn how to use direct access trading tools and master the fundaments? It depends, of course, on whether you are looking to be a day trader, a part-time direct access trader, or simply a long-term direct access trader. Regardless, it does take time to learn the basics, and it also requires a fundamental interest in the financial markets. Like learning anything else, it takes time, but if you have an interest in what you are doing, it is so much easier. And the beauty of direct access trading is that it is designed to provide you with the same tools as the Wall Street professionals. Therefore, over time you have the opportunity to do better than ever before with your investments—whether they are intraday trades or long-terms trades for your retirement. We take a look at a couple of the different scenarios below.

DAY TRADERS

Expectations

The initial trading strategy for a full-time day trader should be to lose as little money as possible. Depending on whether or not you have someone who is going to be training you, as well as their skill set, it almost always takes some time before you can make money in the markets. The first thing to do is to protect your downside. Some of the world's best day traders almost never made it to where they are today because of their setbacks early on. If you have $25,000 of investment capital to trade with in the markets, you must do everything you can to preserve as much as possible in the early stages and then begin steadily growing your capital. This is done by spending as long as a couple of weeks initially using the trading simulator, getting comfortable reading charts, learning the keyboard, and getting familiar with new information such as market maker movements. Regardless of your previous level of investing or trading experience, both individuals with no experience in the financial markets and previous traders at large Wall Street firms have been successful. The key is spending the time early on learning the tools, establishing a strategy, and being very disciplined. It often takes many full-time day traders anywhere from 3 to 6 months to start making money consistently. This is not to say that some do not "get it" much sooner, but there are also those who are just not successful as full-time day traders. Your profit expectations should be extremely low for a considerable period of time, and unless you can afford this personally, you should not do it. After you have achieved your initial goal of at least being positive at the end of every day on a consistent basis, then you can start to move your risk level up a bit. However, if you want to make a consistent living, and possibly a very good living, as a full-time day trader, it is always important to keep your expectations in check. Although there are numerous day traders out there making millions, many of them have an extremely high level of fluctuation in their bank accounts because they make such large trades to get to that level. Many day traders see someone they know make a killing one day and then go out and try to do it themselves the next, completely abandoning their trading strategy. This is what breeds failure. If you can consistently make $2000 a day, with very low risk profiles, you can earn a very nice six-figure income. However, one day of "shooting for the stars" and placing a couple of big trades can ruin an entire month. The key is to always keep your expectations in check and be very disciplined with respect to your trading strategy.

Types of Stocks Traded

Day traders tend to trade highly volatile stocks, such as technology stocks, in order to take advantage of the big movements. For day traders, volatility means the opportunity to make money. Many day traders have a core group of active stocks they trade, and then on a daily basis they review the ten or so most active stocks to see if there are any new stocks they should add to their list to begin trading. Chapter 4 provides a list of possible stocks that less conservative day traders trade. Those taking a more conservative approach to day trading will want to stick with stocks that do not fluctuate as much over the course of a day. It is important, however, to be realistic about the profit potential from trading different types of stocks. Traditionally, stocks priced above $100 a share tend to be much more active than stocks priced below $50 a share. When you start to talk about stocks that are priced less than $10 a share, there is usually even less movement. However, it is very possible that on a daily basis one of these stocks that is priced under $10 a share is going to move as much as one or two times its current trading price—the key is to find out which it could be by following the news. Although this could prove to be an excellent opportunity for day traders comfortable with more risk, conservative day traders would want to steer clear of such stocks. You can realistically expect on a normal basis that the higher the price of a stock, the more it can jump up or down over the course of a day. Just remember, though, Internet stocks have rewritten many traditional trading rules. As long as the Internet continues to receive the same level of attention that it has over the last couple of years, Internet stocks as a group will have the potential to be more volatile than any other group.

Discipline Levels

For full-time day traders, discipline is the most important factor determining whether they will be successful or not. The ability to establish a clear-cut enter and exit strategy—and stick to it—can be the reason for success or failure for almost all day traders. Undisciplined traders get eaten alive in the markets. Professionals are called professionals because they have "survived" longer than the rest—and this is because of their discipline and ability to update and adapt their trading strategies. You can expect that it is not as easy as you might think to stay disciplined all the time. There may be situations in which that you think you are 100 percent sure that a stock will move in a certain way or you are convinced that there is no way a stock can go any lower, but these are the temptations you must resist if you want to succeed as a full-time direct access trader. Resist these temptations at all cost.

Necessary Training

Full-time day trading requires at least a minimal level of training. The best training possible, however, comes from sitting with other more experienced traders. Because most new full-time direct access traders lose money at first, you also need to spend a significant amount of time using simulators. There are also a plethora of additional books and videos available in the marketplace. However, the key is to begin developing your own trading strategy and style. Make sure to allocate at least a month of training to prepare your skills for full-time day trading. For some individuals, it can even take longer. The key is to remain using a simulator until you are comfortable. Lose fake money until you start actually making money on a consistent basis in the simulator. However, no matter how much you practice on a simulator, there is undeniably a difference when you go live and start using real money. The important part, however, is not to think of it this way. If you start thinking about every trade, such as, "I just lost enough money to go on a trip" or "I just made enough money to pay the rent this month," it can be very dangerous. The best full-time direct access traders in the world treat their profits or losses as simply a number on their screen. They are able to mentally block out the fact that their personal net worth is rising and falling every time they make a trade and focus on the task at hand. The key is learning how to block this out as much as possible.

Commitment Necessary

Successful full-time day traders approach trading as a very serious profession, just like being a lawyer or a doctor. They show up every day for work and really love what they do. In fact, you have to love day trading to be successful at it. Even though the market is only open from 9:30 A.M. to 4:30 P.M. EST, these seven hours contain more intensity than most people have packed in a week. Therefore, concentration must be maintained at an extremely high level. People who want to make day trading a professional career need to approach it very seriously from day one. Because so much is happening so quickly on a daily basis, even the shortest mental lapses can prove to be very costly. Especially when starting, it is very helpful to get in early before the markets and analyze upcoming news on the stocks that you trade, and then stay after the market closes and analyze both your winning and losing positions from the day. Full-time direct access trading is actually kind of like having your own business. The brunt of the responsibility falls squarely on your shoulders, and no one is going to do anything to help you. However, there is nothing holding you back, and you can make as much money as your hard work and talent will enable you to make. There is no such thing anywhere as easy money. The most successful full-time day traders in the world who are making millions every year are doing so because they work harder and better than other traders.

Questions to Ask Yourself
1 Do I have enough capital to begin day trading full time?
2 Can I afford to lose all this money?
3 Will I be all right without any income for at least 3 months?
4 Do I have other financial responsibilities that should prevent me from risking this capital?
5 What goals must I achieve on the simulator before I go live and trade real money?
6 Is there someone I know who can help ease me into direct access trading?
7 Am I comfortable with risk?
8 Do I enjoy the fast-paced nature of trading?
9 How long do I want to do this for?
10 What is my backup plan?

PART-TIME DAY TRADERS

The part-time day trader is usually looking to use the direct access trading tools to day trade in certain instances and make longer-term trades in others. He or she probably allocates a certain percentage of his or her overall portfolio to more speculative trading activities such as day trading. It is extremely wise for a part-time trader to *not* use all his or her investment capital for day trading. It is very difficult to pull up a chair at 1:30 P.M. on a trading day and successfully day trade for the remaining part of the day. Because so much of day trading is being in tune with the overall financial markets, most successful day traders recommend that you commit to it full time. However, many individuals do part-time day trading successfully for certain events such as the initial public offering (IPO) of a new stock or for one or two specific stocks they know very well. In addition, part-time traders are able to capitalize on the real-time information and better execution of direct access trading for all their trades. This means that even when they place an order for 1000 shares of Microsoft that they plan on holding for the next 10 years, if they were able to get in at ⅛ point better because of their technology, they just saved an additional $125. Why overpay for a stock when you can check and see if there is a better price available in the marketplace? Over time, this adds up, and the part time trader is able to use his or her knowledge of the markets with real-time news and direct access trading tools to become a better all-around trader. In addition, many individuals who think they might be interested in full-time direct access trading do this at the beginning to see how successful they are with the two or three stocks they day trade.

Types of Stocks
Part-time day traders are usually looking to have as balanced a portfolio as possible. Although they may use a certain percentage of their investment capital to day trade, by having the rest of their money in other longer-term investments, they considerably lessen their overall risk. It is important, even as a part-time day trader, to stick with your longer-term investments. It can be very tempting, especially with the tools to enter and exit trades so quickly, to abandon stocks that are diving or escalating rapidly in the markets. The key is to stick to your trading strategy as closely as possible. Part-time traders who day trade usually do so only with a couple of stocks. It is important to select anywhere from two to five stocks that you can want to day trade and can monitor on a daily basis. Even though you will not actually be trading them on a daily basis, it is important to monitor things such as their stock chart and their reaction to specific pieces of news so that when you do sit down to day

trade them, you are much more in tune with what is happening. Trying to sit down and day trade stocks that you have not researched or traded in the past is a recipe for disaster. It is important to realize that because you are only day trading part time, you must lessen your expectations about what level of success you will have. Over time you should get more and more comfortable with the stocks that you are trading and be able to take larger positions if this fits in with your trading strategy.

Discipline

Discipline is the most important element for all traders, but especially for part-time direct access traders who are making both intraday trades and longer-term traders. This is so because there is in essence two sets of discipline at work—one for your day trading and another for your longer-term investments. It is important to clearly differentiate the two as much as possible. In fact, it is usually a good idea to put on only one hat every time you sit down to trade. If you are going to day trade, then only day trade during that trading session. If you are at your computer wanting to just research stocks and investigate longer-term buys, refrain from day trading. Keeping the two different trading strategies as separate as possible will help ingrain discipline that much more.

Necessary Training

As a part-time day trader, you can definitely expect to need a substantial amount of training. Because potentially you are going to be day trading full time, it is important to understand all the elements of day trading as well as to master the new direct access trading tools. Almost always it is a good idea to start out with longer-term trading for the first couple of months before making the transition to learning day trading. During this time, you can master the keyboard, begin to understand level II quotes, start learning market maker movements, and begin developing the couple of stocks you plan to day trade. However, even before you place your first long-term trade using direct access trading tools, it is important to spend some time on a simulator. This will enable you to get comfortable with the look and feel of the trading screen and the plethora of new information on your screen. Expect to spend at least a week or two practicing on a simulator before "going live" with your first real trade. Perhaps the most time-consuming thing will be getting accustomed to the keyboard and the proper keystrokes to place trades.

Commitment Necessary

Becoming a part-time day trader requires an ongoing commitment to and interest in the financial markets. Although all part-time day traders should start out on a simulator well before they actually start day trading for real, most find it second nature after a while to place even their longer-term trades this way. However, because part-time day traders make intra-day trades as well, they are subject to many of the same responsibilities that day traders have. For instance, full-time day traders spend all day looking at various stocks, placing trades, and interpreting overall market sentiment. As a part-time day trader, there is no way for you to realistically follow as many stocks, but you must keep up to date with the stocks you do day trade on a daily basis. The way a stock moves every day is another clue to interpreting and predicting its movement over time. Only by pulling up the intraday chart and looking at the way the stock reacted to stock-specific news, general market news, and market maker movements will you be able to get a true feeling for the "personality" of a stock. Successful direct access traders are extremely committed to always improving their understanding of the markets and updating their trading strategy. If you are just using direct access trading tools to place longer-term trades, then a far lower level of commitment is necessary (once you have mastered the fundamentals) than if you are day trading as well.

Questions to Ask Yourself

1 What do I expect to gain from using direct access trading tools?
2 How comfortable am I with the fast-paced nature of direct access trading?
3 How much experience do I have with the markets?
4 Is there someone I know who can help ease me into direct access trading?
5 What goals must I achieve on the simulator before I go live and trade real money?
6 How much of my investment capital am I going to devote to day trading?
7 Which stocks am I going to day trade?
8 Can I afford to lose all this money?
9 Do I have other financial responsibilities that should prevent me from risking this capital?
10 Do I enjoy the fast-paced nature of trading?

LONG-TERM DIRECT ACCESS TRADERS

More and more we will see online investors begin using direct access trading tools. Regardless of how many trades individuals place over the course of a year, direct access trading tools allow everyone to access the markets directly and get in and out of stocks at the best possible price. Why lose an extra ⅛ point every time you enter and exit an investment because you were not aware of a better price being offered. In addition, why not be able to see the same information that Wall Street professionals use every time they place a trade? Almost 90 percent of online investors are unaware that level II quotes even exist. Almost 95 percent of online investors have never even heard of market makers. These two items specifically are the backbone of information that professional traders use when deciding when to enter and exit trades. Now that the tools are available to online investors and are packaged in an easier-to-use way than ever before possible, the online investor can take advantage of the same tools Wall Street professionals have used for years. For online investors, the first thing to do is to get comfortable with the abundance of new information available. Everything from level II quotes to market maker movements requires a little understanding. A little later on in this book we explain some of the basics. The initial strategy for an online investor getting into using direct access trading tools should be to get the best possible price for every trade made and to begin getting an understanding of the new information available. Regardless of how little money or how few trades you place, getting an understanding of the technology now will help you excel in the markets as your portfolio grows. Direct access trading tools are the way of the future—the not so distant future, where those who are comfortable with its capabilities will be able to capitalize on the many new investment opportunities worldwide. Online investors who spend the time to learn now will be able to capitalize early on opportunities in the future.

Types of Stocks

There is no extra risk in trading specific types of stocks for individuals who use direct access trading tools simply to place their normal longer-term trades. The stocks you purchase still carry the same levels of risk as if you bought them through a broker. Just because you are using direct access trading tools does not make the purchase any riskier. In fact, direct access trading tools will allow you to get in and out of stocks much more quickly than ever before possible. Whether it is a hot IPO that you would normally have had to place a market order to get in on or a rapidly declining stock that you want to get out of immediately, direct access trading tools will give you an edge over every individual using an online or other type of broker. Therefore, direct access trading tools simply give you an edge when trading any type of stock once you have mastered how to use them.

Discipline

The discipline required for long-term direct access traders is basically no different from that for traditional online investors. The only trap that some long-term direct access traders fall into is the desire to use direct access trading tools to make uneducated buying and selling decisions on impulse. Because the tools are so powerful and so "real time," it is important not to get caught up in the capabilities that direct access trading tools provide. If your trading strategy is to be a long-term direct access trader, do not decide to be a day trader one day just because you feel like it. If you think you want to get into shorter-term trading, such as day trading, re-adjust your trading strategy and goals accordingly before jumping into it. Otherwise, stick to your game plan and remain disciplined at all times.

Necessary Training

Every individual who gets into direct access trading needs at least some level of training. Even if you think you are an expert in the markets, spend some time on a simulator and read a book or two on direct access trading before thinking about going live. The act of buying and selling stocks is still the same, but the way you do that is very different. In addition, because there is no "undo" button, it is critical to make sure you get every trade right. This means getting comfortable on the keyboard, knowing your ticker symbols, and understanding the shortcuts to placing trades even more quickly. There are also numerous seminars and electronic trading firms that offer education classes for new electronic traders. We have found, however, that most of these are oriented toward day traders specifically and not toward individuals interested in using direct access trading tools for placing their longer-term trades. This book is just the first step in learning direct access trading. The other books in this series are a great way to learn more about direct access trading, as well as using a simulator, as on Tradescape.com.

Commitment Necessary

Deciding to use direct access trading tools requires a commitment to learn how to use this new technology. Placing direct access trades is very different from placing a third-party trade with an online broker. It takes a little while to get comfortable with your new tools and real-time information. In addition, there is now a plethora of information flashing in different colors across your screen that you need to be able to understand. Do not be intimidated by the abundance of information. You eventually can customize it to exactly what you want to see. For now, you just need to dedicate yourself to spending some time to learn the fundamentals. Since you have already bought this book, you are well underway. And once you have mastered the fundamentals, you will wonder how you ever traded before.

Questions to Ask Yourself

1   What do I expect to gain from using direct access trading tools?
2   How comfortable am I with the fast-paced nature of direct access trading?
3   How much experience do I have with the markets?
4   What are the areas I am going to need the most help on learning (keyboard, market makers, level II quotes)?
5   What goals must I achieve on the simulator before I go live and trade real money?
6   Am I going to ever make any intraday trades?
7   What is my previous experience with trading?

C H A P 3 T E R

DEVELOPING A TRADING STRATEGY

If you are going to trade successfully, it is imperative that you have a trading strategy. Whether you make one trade a year or a hundred trades a day, you must outline your trading goals and expectations on a regular basis. Only by identifying these goals can you truly maximize your investment capital. Without a trading strategy, you are much more likely to succumb to the whims of emotion that are the downfall of most unsuccessful direct access traders. Most direct access traders update their trading strategies based on their goals and the frequency with which they trade.

Developing a trading strategy is essentially based on identifying your risk-reward comfort levels. Each direct access trader has different goals. Some are looking to trade as a full-time profession. Others just want to take advantage of the cutting-edge technology that allows access to greater amounts of information and the ability to get the best possible price on every trade. Your trading strategy is also highly dependent on the amount of capital you have to invest in the marketplace. The old adage "only put money in the stock market that you can afford to lose" still holds true. Obviously, the risk level differs if you are day trading an extremely volatile technology stock or placing trades in blue chip stocks that do not move as much. However, all these factors need to be taken into consideration from day one.

DISCIPLINE

Discipline is the most important skill for all direct access traders. Anyone can say they have developed a trading strategy, but only those who stick to it religiously will be truly successful. More important, strict discipline also offers the greatest amount of downside protection. For example, if you are a day trader, you may make a rule that you will not lose more than $2000 on any given trade. Therefore, if you buy 1000 shares of stock XYZ at $100 and it goes down 2 points, regardless of what you think is going to happen next, you cut your losses and move on. More people lose their shirts waiting for a losing position to come back up than anything else. On the upside, you may make a rule that if a stock goes up by a certain amount, you will sell a certain number of shares to lock in your gain and then let the remaining shares run until there is a certain point decline.

For those who are using the direct access trading technology for longer-term positions, the same holds true. Every stock is subject to ups and downs over the course of a day, week, month, or year. If your research leads you to believe that your stock is a good pick for the time period for which you have developed your trading strategy, and no news comes out to persuade you otherwise, stick with it. Do not sell a stock just because it is down 2 points on a day when the market is not doing well and all stocks are down or if you see a handful of technology stocks up 10 points in a day and yours is not moving nearly as quickly.

Discipline is of the utmost importance for all direct access traders. Everyone is subject to whims and impulses; however, those who stay true to their initial trading strategy have a far greater chance of success than those who do not.

THE RISK SPECTRUM

Direct access trading can be as risky or conservative as you want to make it. The technology behind direct access trading allows you to become a better investor or trader at any level. The technology is ideal for both day traders and long-term investors. Regardless of how you use the direct access trading technology, the risks involved are similar to those associated with an online brokerage firm. However, there are definitely clear advantages to using direct access technology. For example, once you are comfortable using the new set of investing tools, you will be able to enter and exit trades much more quickly than ever before possible. Therefore, if the market is tanking and you want to get out of your position immediately, there is no waiting for confirmation from your broker. When you place your sell order, you are out—instantly. Also, if you want to try to get in shortly after the initial public offering (IPO) of a stock, you will be able to do so much more quickly—and at the price you specify— by using the direct access trading technology as opposed to placing a market order through an online broker.

There are certain new risks that need to be considered, though. For example, the interface for direct access trading is not yet "as convenient" as placing a trade through an online broker. There are no reminders to double-check your order, and there is no "undo" button. When you hit "Enter" to place a trade, it happens instantaneously. Therefore, as we will discuss later, it is extremely important to become comfortable on the keyboard and master your keystrokes so that you can execute trades effortlessly. This is obviously much more important if you are a day trader. Nonetheless, all users must be able to execute trades using the same functions. Now let's take a look at the various risk levels associated with different groups of direct access traders.

At one end of the risk spectrum you have day traders. Day trading can be an extremely risky proposition for anyone, yet the rewards are potentially the greatest as well. Day traders often trade significant blocks of stock (usually in round lots of 100 and up) in hopes that the price will rise $1/16$ or $1/8$ ("teenies") so that they can make a quick profit. Conversely, the stock also can drop very quickly. Fortunately for day traders, the technology of direct access trading allows them to enter and exit trades instantaneously. For day traders in particular, mastering the keyboard is a must. They must be able to effortlessly glide from screen to screen and trade to trade in order to stay on top of their capital in the marketplace. Because they may only be in a trade for a matter of seconds, it is crucial that they make clean keystrokes with no errors. As we will discuss later, anyone who wants to get into day trading should spend at least a week mastering the keyboard and practicing making trades on a simulation system. The last thing anyone wants is to own (or sell) a block of shares erroneously. There are plenty of horror stories about day traders who have lost everything. If these traders had established a trading strategy from day one, however, their stories would be quite different. It is the individuals who jump into day trading blindly, expecting to make millions within their first 3 months, who are susceptible to the highest losses.

Even if you are a day trader, there are ways to mitigate your risk. As will be demonstrated later, there are certain stocks that are apt to move much less over the course of a trading day than others. In addition, using some of your capital to make other types of investments and diversifying your overall portfolio can be very helpful. Day trading is inherently the most risky way to capitalize on direct access execution. However, by identifying your trading goals from the start and staying disciplined, you will greatly increase your odds for success.

At the other end of the spectrum you have online investors who are using the direct access trading technology to place all their trades. The risks involved in placing a trade with an online broker and using direct access tools are almost identical, with a couple of key exceptions. First, with direct access technology, there is no confirmation or double-check of your order screen. When you hit "Enter," you are in essence buying or selling directly from another individual at a computer somewhere else. The trade is executed immediately. It is also immediately undoable. On the flip side, there is no waiting to find out when your order was executed and at what price. Therefore, when you see the price you want, you can get it immediately. Although the direct access trading tools still look a bit strange to online investors making the jump, over time they will become much more user friendly.

WHY ESTABLISH A TRADING STRATEGY?

A trading strategy is what helps direct access traders take the emotion out of trading. They are able to focus on the market and make their trades instinctively, instead of letting emotions enter the picture. Traders who stick to their trading strategies over time have the greatest chances for success. However, coming up with a trading strategy that fits your personal goals and risk profile is the difficult part. The next couple of pages will show you some examples of how to do just this.

WHEN TO LET A STOCK GO

There comes a point in every trader's life when a stock he or she "loves" just does not make money any more. Traders like to trade stocks they have made money with in the past. Of course, this is no surprise, but sometimes the "personality" of a stock changes so dramatically that traders lose their feel for trading that particular stock. This should not be taken personally. You should trade stocks that will make you money. It is this simple. If you find that you are consistently losing money on a stock that you cannot understand, move on. How quickly you move on once again goes back to your goals. If you are a day trader and you consistently lose money on a stock over the course of a week, maybe it is time to focus on another stock. The main issue focuses more on your technical analysis of the stock than on any fundamentals. If you are a longer-term direct access trader, then your decision really depends more on the fundamentals of the particular stock. What has changed with respect to this particular stock that is making the price go down? One of the main advantages direct access traders have is that if the price is plummeting rapidly, they can exit their trade quickly. However, if a stock is going down gradually, then it becomes more of a gut feeling for traders on when to exit the position. The bottom line is that direct access trading is meant to make money. Outline in your goals how much downside you are willing to take on any position—and act accordingly.

HOW TO GET READY TO TRADE A STOCK

No type of direct access trader should ever just jump into trading any particular stock. Trading a stock without having done your homework is very much like gambling. However, when you do your own research and make trading decisions based on your goals, you are putting the odds much more in your own favor. For day traders, it is important to analyze the historical charts for a particular stock and get to know who the major market makers within the stock are. It is also important to analyze historical trends and what caused significant moves in the price of the stock. The amount of time day traders spend analyzing stocks they may trade runs the gamut. Some do their research either before the market opens or after it closes, whereas others do it on the fly during the course of the day. Those who do their research more on the fly, however, are day trading veterans who have done it for quite some time and know exactly what they are looking for. For others, especially new day traders, it is highly advisable to do your research outside market hours. For longer-term direct access traders, it is more important to study such things as research reports and other fundamental analyses with regard to the stock. Analyst predictions on share price also can be very useful, unless they are for Internet stocks, which have proven to be a shot in the dark more than anything else. As a long-term direct access trader, you are studying the fundamentals of the company, which will hopefully give you insight into what the share price of the stock will be over time. However, having access to direct access trading tools means that you have the ability to capitalize on new opportunities as they develop with respect to your stocks. Therefore, you should look at charts as well to understand what has made the share price spike substantially up or down in the past. Using direct access trading, you may be able to purchase additional shares of stock if it hits a bottom over the course of a day or even sell shares of stock one day if the stock has reached a new high and then get back in at a later point once the price has subsided. Having direct access trading tools allows you to trade the stock as well as invest in it. It is up to you how much activity you want to have with respect to buying and selling it, but the tools will be there if you decide to do so.

EVALUATING YOUR TRADES

It is extremely important to evaluate your trades on a consistent basis. This is where you can get a very good understanding of your trading patterns and what is working well and not working for you. You must evaluate both your winning and losing trades. You do not have to analyze every one of your trades, but only by going back and looking at what you did will you be able to learn in the future. Although the markets are always changing, you will be able especially to see patterns in your trading style, which should help you update your strategy and your goals. As a day trader, you should evaluate your trades on a daily basis. Especially when you are just starting, it is a good idea to also see if any other experienced traders happened to trade the same stock you did over the course of the day. Look at their position charts and get them to explain what they saw in the markets and why they bought and sold the way they did. Ask yourself such questions as

- Why did I not hold onto a trade longer?
- Why did I not sell this position at this point?
- What stock did I do the best on today?
- What stock did I do the worst on today?
- What sort of patterns did I see emerging in this stock today?
- What market makers were particularly active?

For longer-term direct access traders, it is smart to examine your trades on a weekly, monthly, or quarterly basis depending on how frequently you are trading. If you are making multiple trades a week, then examine them weekly, and if you are making multiple trades a month, then examine them monthly, and so on. Keep a special eye out for opportunities you may have missed over that time to trade the stock. Ask yourself such questions as

- What were the events that made the stock price spike on that particular day?
- Would it have been a good opportunity to trade the stock?
- What stocks have I done particularly well with?
- What stocks have I lost money on?
- What patterns have emerged that I could possibly use to make money on in the future?
- How successful would I have been if I did not trade the stock at all over the course of this time period?

There are clues everywhere with respect to how a stock price fluctuates. There also will be times when there really is no concrete answer as to why a stock acted the way it did. Learn what you can from evaluating your trades, but mostly focus on taking away things that can help you in making better trades in the future. Evaluating trades is a step that a lot of both investors and traders tend to skip, especially when they are making money. The markets are changing all the time, and in order to stay on top of things, you need to evaluate your trades.

ESTABLISHING YOUR INITIAL TRADING STRATEGY

The first thing to do when establishing your trading strategy is to analyze how much money you have to trade with and how much you can *really* afford to lose. Then you should examine your long-term personal goals. Both these factors will affect what your risk-reward scenario should be. Whether you plan to become a day trader or you want to use the direct access trading technology to make better longer-term trades, the jump to direct access will require a little adapting. It is highly recommended that anyone starting out in direct access trading practice on a simulator first. This can be done online at *www.tradescape.com,* for example. "Trading" without risk will help you get the feel for direct access trading. It does have a different look and feel from any other form of investing. Regardless of whether you want to become a full-time day trader, a part-time trader, or a general investor, it is always wise to start on the more conservative side. This means establishing downside protections. Direct access traders who take the time in the beginning to establish a trading strategy raise their chances for success exponentially. Successful traders review their trading strategy every day before they trade.

A rules-based approach to direct access trading can be your best ally. By establishing your rules in the beginning, based on your trading strategy, you can minimize to an extent the effect that emotions will have on your trades. All the most successful direct access traders in the world have rules. In fact, their rules are so embedded in their brains that they do not even have to think about them when they are trading. They just react instantaneously. Because speed is so critical for direct access traders, it is important that your rules become second nature.

Let's take a look at a couple of different direct access traders and what their trading strategies might look like.

Full-time day trader

1 I will practice on the simulator until I start making a handful of winning trades on a frequent basis and am 100 percent comfortable on the keyboard and with the information I need to interpret to be successful.

2 I will arrive at least an hour before the markets open in the morning to get prepared mentally.

3 I will try to find a mentor to help me better understand full-time day trading.

4 I will not lose more than 25 percent of my trading capital in the first month of real trading.

5 I will never lose more than 5 percent of my trading capital on any given day.

6 I will get out of losing positions after being down more than $500.

7 I will never risk more than 10 percent of my capital on any individual trade.

8 I will sell off a percentage of my position when I have a trade that is in the money so that I cover my investment. I will then remain in the position until it ticks down more than 1 point.

9 I will consistently have positive days after the second month of real trading.

10 I will examine my winning and losing trades at the end of every day to understand what I did right and what I did wrong.

Part-time day trader

1 I will spend as long as it takes for me to feel comfortable using direct access trading tools on a simulator.

2 I will learn about market maker movements and level II quotes.

3 I will not begin using direct access trading tools until I am completely comfortable on the keyboard.

4 I will only trade IPOs and specific stocks that I watch on a consistent basis.

5 I will only use 25 percent of my investment capital for day trading.

6 I will use the remaining 75 percent of my investment capital in various longer-term positions and will diversify my holdings.

7 I will never pull up a chair in the middle of the trading day and attempt to day trade.

8 I will only day trade when I have done research the night before and conclude that there will be a specific opportunity in a specific stock on the following day.

Long-term direct access trader

1 I will spend as long as it takes for me to feel comfortable using direct access trading tools on a simulator.

2 I will learn about market maker movements and level II quotes.

3 I will not begin using direct access trading tools until I am completely comfortable on the keyboard.

4 I will use direct access trading tools to get in and out of trades at the best price possible.

5 I will use direct access trading tools to learn about the next generation of investing opportunities available in marketplaces around the world.

6 I will stop using direct access trading tools if I am uncomfortable in any way after trying it for at least a month.

UPDATING YOUR STRATEGY

It is important for all direct access traders—day, part-time, and long-term—to update their trading strategies on a frequent basis. The markets are fluctuating more than ever, so every level trader needs to update his or her risk-reward profile on a frequent basis to maximize his or her investment capital.

When updating your trading strategy, it is important to carefully analyze your previous trading strategy and understand what worked well and what did not. This will help you identify your strengths as well as areas on which you need to work. Whether your capital base has doubled or has been cut in half, now it is time to readjust your risk levels in the marketplace accordingly.

Let's take a look at the various types of traders and when it is appropriate for them to update their trading strategies.

Day traders who are making more than a couple of trades every day often need to update their strategies on a weekly basis, if not sooner. For example, if the Federal Reserve (Fed) raises interest rates, there may be no effect on the long-term holders of a stock, but day traders could be affected adversely immediately. Therefore, they need to adjust their strategies after such announcements to reflect the increased risk level they create. Day traders are more affected by stock-specific news and general market news than any other group. Stocks often move as a result of factors other than specific news on a stock. Hence day traders also need to understand what factors will influence such moves and how to get in at the right time. Market conditions change every day.

Some day traders update their trading strategies on a quarterly basis. Some update on a weekly basis. Others update their trading strategies when they feel that the underlying fundamentals of the market, such as entering a bear market, have changed. Each individual day trader is a bit different; however, each needs to keep a finger on the pulse of the markets to understand when the time has come to tweak his or her strategy. The most successful day traders in the world are the ones who have been doing it for the longest time. They are the ones who have proven their ability to change with the markets. These day traders can make money in any type of market because they are able to stay in tune with the market.

The trading strategy for part-time day traders and direct access traders who are making a couple of trades a week is very different. These direct access traders must monitor both the general market sentiments and longer-term trends of the stocks they are holding. Part-time day traders in particular must reexamine their trading strategies on a weekly, if not daily, basis (on days on which they trade). Because they are not in touch with the markets on a daily basis, as full-time day traders are, it is almost always more difficult for them to interpret the effects of general market movements and trends. Part-time day traders realistically should only be trading a couple of stocks that they know very well and can monitor on a more frequent basis. It is important that they understand what other market factors and trends can affect the short-term movements of those individual stocks. Therefore, part-time day traders need to find ways to at least monitor the individual stocks they trade on a frequent basis in order to understand how the stock reacted to certain pieces of news and what market makers and other groups were actively trading the stock.

In addition, part-time day traders need to update their strategies based on how much time they are going to be able to devote to direct access trading. If you know that you are going to be away for a month and completely out of touch with the markets, you should drastically cut your risk levels when you return because it will take you some time to get back in the groove. In addition, before you leave, you may even want to liquidate any longer-term positions you are holding that you do not want to leave in the market for whatever reason.

Direct access traders who are making longer-term investments and using the technology for better information and lower prices need to adjust their trading strategies just like any other long-term investor. It is a good idea for such traders to reexamine their trading strategies on a quarterly or semiannual basis—and even sooner if there is a huge up- or downswing in the markets. One of the major upsides to using direct access trading technology for long-term investors is the ability to enter and exit trades in real time, rather than waiting as you do when you place a trade through a third party. Therefore, if the market were to take a nosedive, you would be able to exit your positions much more quickly than ever before. Although long-term direct access traders do not need to update their trading strategies as often as both full- and part-time day traders, it is imperative that they maintain a watchful eye over the markets in general so that they can react if the market makes a drastic movement. Although long-term investors using direct access trading technology are in the minority right now, their numbers will climb steadily over the next few years. As the Internet continues to level the playing field in the online investing world and companies create more user-friendly interfaces for investors of all levels to capitalize on the technology, direct access trading will become the standard.

The markets fluctuate more than ever. It is now imperative for everyone to regularly review their trading strategy. In addition, whether you are a full-time day trader or a long-term investor, it is important for you to have a mix of holdings in your portfolio. These holdings should be in a variety of industries, and at least some portion of them should be in longer-term investments. It is not wise for anyone to trade with all the capital they have.

Updating one's trading strategy is about surviving and thriving over the long term. Anyone can have a good quarter or a good year. Successful traders are the ones who do this year after year. As with any other activity, in order to stay on top of your game, you have to keep improving and adapting. Those traders who regularly update their trading strategies and diversify their holdings stand the greatest chance for success over the long term.

MARKET INDICATORS

All types of direct access traders must watch general market indicators and stock-specific market indicators to get a feeling for the direction their stocks are heading. Remember, just because you may own the greatest stock in the world that just achieved record revenues and profitability, there is no guarantee that its price will go up (at least in the short term). General market effects such as inflation numbers, the Fed raising interest rates, and a perceived bull or bear market will influence all stocks. Therefore, it is important for all direct access traders to stay abreast of overall market activities. Stock-specific indicators include earnings reports, research report upgrades and downgrades, acquisitions, key hires and fires, product releases, and any other significant pieces of news that will affect your position. Also remember that if you own an Internet stock, for example, it is quite possible that the stock is receiving heightened attention for a specific reason. Even if the stock is just in the next "hot area" of the Internet, this can play a significant role in increasing its price. Also remember that day traders especially rely much more on technical analysis than on fundamental news. Although they will monitor fundamental news, they use it more as an indicator for which stocks to watch and then use technical analysis to make their trading decisions.

KNOWING WHICH STOCKS TO TRADE

Everyone knows that there are thousands of ways to invest your money in the stock market. You can invest in a plethora of different stocks, all of which have their own unique characteristics and risk profiles. By analyzing such data as historical charts, you can get a sense of the volume level in a stock and where the stock price has been over any period of time. In addition, certain market factors will affect the prices of all stocks. These include activities by the Fed, war, and general market trends, just to name a few. Depending on what type of direct access trader you are, there are certain stocks that will be better suited to your risk-reward profile. Everyone is best served over the long term by having a diverse portfolio. However, over time, every stock goes in and out of favor. Therefore, by consistently knowing which stocks are in favor, you will be able to adjust your risk-reward profile and update your portfolio.

Mastering direct access trading fundamentals is just one part of the equation. The next is to understand which stocks to use your newfound skills on. Just remember that gains can be made on any stock. In fact, many traders have made their biggest gains on stocks no one had ever heard of at the time. By understanding what to look at, where to look, and how to capitalize on a specific stock when you find it, you can greatly increase your profits in direct access trading.

The first thing to examine in any stock is its volatility. This can be determined by looking at a historical chart that shows the stock price over a specific period of time. It is generally a good idea to analyze at least the previous year but preferably longer as well. Remember that certain industries are prone to more movement than others. Do not rule out industries where there appears to be little movement; they can be some of the best areas to get your experience in direct access trading. Volatility is the best measure of how risky a stock is. Internet stocks, for

TABLE 3-1.   MOST HEAVILY TRADED STOCKS FOR 6/13/00
JDSU
ATHM
LCOS
ITWO
CMGI
SEBL
SDLI
JNPR
AMCC
ELON

example, have been known to double or even triple on their first day of trading, making them some of the riskiest stocks to own both long and short term. When assessing volatility, look not only at the number of points a stock moved but also at the movement's percentage of the overall stock price. For example, a stock that goes from $2 a share to $6 a share over the course of a day is a more volatile stock than one that goes from $200 a share to $500 a share. If you were to have invested the same $200 in each, you would have made $600 in the first scenario and $500 in the second. Look at percentages, not just point movements.

The next key indicator to examine is the volume of shares being traded. Liquidity is what allows everyone to coexist in the stock market. Without liquidity, our markets would dry up. Stocks that have a higher volume are easier to get in and out of. Volume for every stock fluctuates on a daily basis. However, over any given period of time, there is a core group of stocks that are the most heavily traded. For example, Table 3-1 shows the most heavily traded stocks for June 13, 2000, at Tradescape.com.

Remember, stocks that are priced under $50 a share are usually traded less than stocks priced more than this. Especially when you get into stocks that trade below $10 a share, it is extremely important to analyze the volume of shares being traded. If the volume has declined steadily and leveled off at an all-time low, it could be a risky stock to own shares in. You may end up having trouble unloading them at some point in the future (or at least in the time period you want to do so). On the other hand, if you see an inexpensive stock that has recent spikes in the number of shares being traded, this may prove to be an excellent buying opportunity.

Another way to decide which stocks to trade is simply by industry. Some direct access traders only like to trade Internet stocks, whereas others shy away from them because of their volatility. Industries such as biotechnology have come in and out of favor over time. Most part- and full-time day traders look for the industries that have the most volatility— but not at the beginning. Only after they have mastered the direct access trading tools and are comfortable in the markets do they move on to these stocks. It is much more common for new direct access traders to start out with less volatile stocks. Nevertheless, a lot of traders stick strictly with one industry so that they can follow information on that industry much more closely. For short-term traders this can be a very good strategy. For longer-term trades, though, you should diversify your holdings into different industries.

Many direct access traders also rely on their fellow traders for tips and insights into exciting new stocks. Because there are thousands of stocks to cover, it is impossible for any one individual to cover more than a handful. Therefore, it can be extremely valuable to have a group of individuals you trade with or at least communicate with on a regular basis. Some traders even check the chat rooms on sites such as Yahoo Finance to see which stocks are being discussed the most. Although chat rooms are not "reliable" sources of information by any means, it can be interesting to get a cross section of thoughts on various stocks. A lot of individuals also subscribe to various market recap services that give their opinions on stocks to own. CNBC is an invaluable resource for traders at all levels. Stocks mentioned throughout the day on CNBC usually represent stocks worth checking out. Nonetheless, a group of other traders around you often serves as the best source of information for possible new stocks to trade.

Some direct access traders trade only IPOs. This is perhaps one of the highlights of the advantages of using direct access trading tools. The classic example is the online investor who is at home patiently waiting to find out if his or her trade has been executed and at what price in a new IPO. If the trader specified a price, there is a good chance that he or she may not get in on the trade. Yet, if the trader placed a market order, he or she is subject to the whims of the stock and could end up paying three times the IPO price. With direct access trading tools, however, this same individual can go in the second the stock goes public, find another buyer, and make the purchase instantaneously. The access to real-time information and trading tools is a significant advantage, especially for individuals who are interested in getting in on IPOs. Some direct access traders use the technology for this reason only.

DEVELOPING A CORE GROUP OF STOCKS

The reason every direct access trader has a core group of stocks is that there are simply so many stocks in existence that it is impossible to follow them all. Trying to follow too many stocks is a recipe for disaster. However, "putting your feelers out" in terms of up and coming stocks that may interest you is very important. Successful direct access traders have different ways of monitoring various statistics and news sources to find out about hot new stocks. One approach is simply to look at the list of most active shares traded for individual stocks over the course of a day. Another is to look at the biggest price moves as a percentage of total value over the course of a day, month, or quarter. Finally, it is always a good idea to keep an eye on traditional news sources such as CNBC, the *Wall Street Journal, Investors Business Daily,* and other more traditional sources that do some of the homework for you in terms of pinpointing new up-and-comers.

Because the stock market is moving in unprecedented swings, it is more important than ever to frequently update your core group of stocks. This may mean raising or lowering positions you have in longer-term investments. It may mean identifying new opportunities for shorter-term trades based on emerging industry trends. The key is to stay in sync with the market. The old adage about putting $100 in a blue chip stock and watching what happens to it over 20 years is still true to some extent. However, by keeping an ear to the markets, it is possible to do two, three, even ten times better than this. The key is to follow the markets and get a feel for where they are heading based on your trading strategy. Obviously, if you are a longer-term direct access trader, you will update your core group of stocks much less frequently than a day trader. Day traders should update their core group of stocks weekly, if not daily.

Every direct access trader has a core group of stocks that he or she monitors and trades. Although the mix of stocks can change frequently, there are specific reasons why these types of stocks are chosen. For example, day traders usually look for highly volatile stocks, whereas longer-term direct access traders aim to diversify their portfolios with some riskier stocks and others that will move more gradually. Longer-term direct access traders are normally looking at stocks they expect will grow steadily over time.

As new trends appear and analysts voice their upgrade and downgrade recommendations, stocks naturally fade in and out of favor. Just because a particular stock had a bad day does not mean you sell it. For day traders, this may be the perfect opportunity to buy more. For long-term direct access traders, it is important to watch the overall trends affecting the marketplace, not just a day's individual movements. However, if you do see a trend emerging that could affect your position over the long term, this may be the time to replace such a stock with another one. Successful direct access traders of all types are constantly analyzing their holdings, monitoring potential new stocks to own, and getting a feel for the overall trends affecting the marketplace.

Different stocks in the same industry tend to share similar characteristics, most notably volatility. Although there will always be varying degrees, stocks in the technology industry are generally much more prone to volatility than banking stocks. When developing your core group of stocks, it is important to analyze the various forces at work within particular industries. For example, if a stock is in the Internet industry, its range is going to be significantly wider than most other stocks. Take a look at the stock of Fatbrain (NASD: FATB) over the course of March to June 2000. In just 3 months the stock went from approximately 17 to a low of 4⅛, losing almost all its trading value. Another example is Amazon.com, which had a 52-week high of 113 and a 52-week low of 40⁷⁄₁₆ of June 13, 2000. However, the stock is now virtually at the same price it was a year ago. In addition, because the volume of shares being traded is so significant on this stock, there were numerous days when the stock fluctuated a large number of points. For experienced day traders, this would be a great stock to play. Obviously, the Internet sector is one of the most volatile industries and presents one of the best opportunities for reward. However, for new direct access traders looking to make intraday trades, this is not the area in which to start. Because things are moving so quickly and there is so much volume, it is a very dangerous area in which to begin learning.

Example A: Jake Edwards (experienced full-time day trader)
Risk profile: Risky

Jake should develop a core group of stocks that are going to be the most volatile over the course of a day. Because he has over 6 months of profitable day trading under his belt, he is looking for the stocks that are going to give him the most profit potential. He is comfortable taking on a certain heightened level of risk to achieve his goals. At the end of every trading day, Jake pulls up the list of most active stocks traded for that day to find out if there are any new stocks he should be trading. He updates his core group of stocks on a weekly basis unless he finds a new highly active stock or there is extremely big unanticipated news released on a particular stock. Possible stocks Jake should trade include

QCOM	Qualcomm
EXDS	Exodus
JDSU	JDS Uniphase
AMZN	Amazon.com
YHOO	Yahoo!
PMCS	PMC-Sierra
ORCL	Oracle
BRCM	Broadcom
SDLI	SDL
SUNW	Sun Microsystems
AMAT	Applied Materials

Example B: Jon Pirone (new day trader)
Risk profile: Conservative

Jon should develop a core group of stocks that are not extremely volatile over the course of a trading day. These normally would be stocks that are trading at less than $50 a share and have a trading range no greater than 25 percent of the stock price over the last few quarters. Ideally, Jon should look for stocks that are moving a couple of points a day at most. This will ensure that his downside potential will be very slim. As Jon gets more comfortable trading these types of stocks, he probably will want to practice again on a trading simulator with more volatile stocks instead of just jumping right in. Possible stocks Jon should trade include

TSFM	24/7 Media
FLWS	1–800-Flowers.com
ANF	Abercrombie & Fitch

COMS	3com Corp
BULV	Bulova Corp
SVEV	7-Eleven Corp
AEN	AMC Entertainment
AEOS	American Eagle Outfitters
BOUT	About.com
AGE	A. G. Edwards

Example C: Jason Reed (part-time day trader)
Risk profile: Conservative

Jason should develop a very narrow group of stocks that he can monitor on a frequent basis, even though he may only be trading on a part-time basis. Successful part-time day traders keep a finger on the pulse of the stocks they trade on a very frequent basis. Much of day trading is based on "understanding the personality of a stock." It is unrealistic to think you will make money if you are only monitoring stocks on days on which you are trading. Therefore, Jason must find a couple of stocks that are fairly volatile and that he is comfortable monitoring on a frequent basis. If Jason is consistently losing money on one of the stocks he is trading in particular, he may want to replace that stock with a new one. This can happen over time, especially if he is not consistent in monitoring the activities of one of his stocks. When he does take on a new stock to trade, it is important for him to spend some time watching the stock, if possible using a trading simulator, before actually trading it. Possible stocks for Jason to trade would be three to five of the following, depending on how much time he plans to devote to trading and his comfort level in monitoring multiple stocks:

SAPE	Sapient
YHOO	Yahoo!
NSOL	Network Solutions
HIT	Hitachi
IBM	International Business Machines
HWP	Hewlett-Packard
FDRY	Foundry Networks

JDSU   JDS Uniphase
SCMR   Sycamore Networks

Example D: Jennifer Pollock (new long-term direct access trader)

Risk profile: Extremely conservative

Jennifer should develop a core group of stocks that will be good investments over the long term. Using direct access trading tools, Jennifer will be able to enter and exit her trades at better prices, have access to more information on the stocks she trades, and be able to capitalize on features of direct access trading such as getting in on IPOs or quickly exiting a stock if an extreme downturn is expected. Jennifer will be more concerned with the long-term opportunity of owning a specific stock than with the price at which that stock is presently trading. For example, eclipsing $100 a share numerous times over the last couple of years, Cisco has seemed expensive to many traders. However, every time the stock splits, owners receive double the number of shares. Long-term direct access traders should be more concerned with owning the stocks they feel will achieve the greatest value in the long term rather than with what price the stock is at or the volume of shares being traded. They should still analyze the volatility to ensure that they understand the swings with which the stock is capable of moving. For Jennifer, buying the blue chip stocks of today and a couple of technology stocks is probably the best way to go. Possible stocks Jennifer should own include

CSCO   Cisco Systems
MSFT   Microsoft
DELL   Dell Computers
GE   General Electric
WMT   Wal-Mart
AOL   America Online
ORCL   Oracle
PG   Proctor & Gamble
T   AT&T
WCOM   MCI/Worldcom
MRK   Merck

TIMELINE AND GOALS

No one can just jump into direct access trading and be successful immediately. It takes time to learn the new set of tools and master the fundamentals so that you can trade with confidence. In fact, you should quickly be able to trade with more confidence than ever before because of your new set of tools and direct access to the markets. No longer do you have to rely on calling a broker, pulling up a "stale" quote online, or putting in a market order and hoping to get somewhere near your price. You are now your own link to Wall Street, but you must take the proper time to master the fundamentals first. It is a good idea for every new direct access trader to give himself or herself a timeline. This timeline should include goals for each stage of advancement.

For example, Joe Goldberg is completely new to direct access trading. He has invested online but has only recently even heard of an electronic communication network (ECN). Joe wants to start placing all his trades using direct access technology and then decide if he is comfortable making the jump to full- or part-time day trading. Joe also has a fairly exhausting day job and really only has a half hour or so each day in which to study the markets. For Joe, the appropriate timeline and goals would look something like this:

Week 1: Establish my trading strategy and allocate a percentage of my portfolio to begin experimenting with direct access trading. Identify exactly what I am going to use direct access trading for (e.g., IPOs, normal trades, volatile stocks).

Weeks 2 and 3: Analyze the capabilities and features of a direct access trading screen. Make sure to get a clear understanding of the capabilities of each function, and start discerning which tools are going to be the most worthwhile for me to use (e.g., for news feeds). Spend a couple minutes each day practicing my keystrokes on a keyboard.

Weeks 4 through 6: Begin simulation on a direct access trading system for half an hour each day. Spend my lunch placing mock trades to get comfortable with all the functions. Identify which areas I am going to need more time analyzing before I go live.

Week 7: Place my first live trade using long-term direct access trading tools.

Once Joe places his first live trade, he will need to spend at least a couple of months using direct access trading tools to see if he is interested in making the jump to full- or part-time day trading. Because the commitment required to do this is so much greater, it is most important that Joe have a real love of and interest in the markets and can handle the greater stresses associated with day trading.

The following examples look at the goals and timeline for a couple of other individuals—one wanting to get into part-time day trading and the other desiring full-time day trading.

Let's take a look at Jennifer Stein, currently an active online investor who wants to make the jump to part-time day trading. She is very interested in the markets and is comfortable devoting an hour or two each day to learning direct access trading. Jennifer's initial goals will be very similar to Joe's, but she will have to spend a greater amount of time understanding the extra risks associated with day trading and getting to know the core stocks she will be day trading.

> *Week 1:* Establish my trading strategy and allocate a percentage of my portfolio to begin experimenting with direct access trading and another percentage to part-time day trading. Identify exactly what I am going to use direct access trading for (e.g., IPOs, normal trades, volatile stocks, day trading particular stocks).
>
> *Weeks 2 and 3:* Analyze the capabilities and features of a direct access trading screen. Make sure to get a clear understanding of the capabilities of each function, and start discerning which tools are going to be the most worthwhile for me to use (e.g., for news feeds). Spend a couple minutes each day practicing my keystrokes on a keyboard.
>
> *Weeks 4 through 6:* Begin simulation on a direct access trading system for half an hour each day. Spend my lunch placing mock trades to get comfortable with all the functions. Identify which areas I am going to need more time analyzing before I go live for long-term trading. Start analyzing a group of two or three stocks by pulling up their intraday charts on a daily basis and trying to get an understanding for them.
>
> *Week 7:* Place my first long-term trade using long-term direct access trading tools.
>
> *Weeks 8 through 10:* Begin day trading simulation on a direct access trading screen during live market hours. Focus on two or three

stocks, and watch for patterns, specific market maker movements, and other indicators. Go back and analyze my trades to see what I did correctly and incorrectly. Identify my specific day trading goals and guidelines for a longer-term basis.

Week 11: Be ready to engage in day trading a stock when the right opportunity arises.

Jennifer may be ready to engage in her first day trading experience at this point, but it also may take her considerably longer. Depending on the amount of time she actually has to devote to studying her stocks, she should not day trade at all until she is completely comfortable in the markets. Jennifer also should get into day trading very slowly. She should be very conservative regarding how much money she puts into the market and then have very strict guidelines about when she enters and exits a particular trade. Because part-time day trading requires that you learn the fundamentals of direct access trading in addition to the fundamentals of day trading, it requires a significant time commitment.

Lastly, let's take a look at Jared Heinz, who wants to become a full-time day trader. Jared needs to allocate at least 3 to 6 months of not making any money in order to master the fundamentals to become a successful day trader. In fact, Jared should be able to afford to possibly lose all the money with which he starts; otherwise, he should not get into day trading. Day trading is by far the riskiest way to use direct access trading tools, but it is potentially the most profitable as well. The goals for any new day trader are simple—try to lose as little money as possible at first. This is done by starting small, setting realistic goals, and spending a considerable amount of time before going on a day trading simulator. Another invaluable resource for new day traders, if you can find one, is a mentor. Almost all the most successful day traders in the world have had a mentor. Although at some point, and often fairly soon after they started, they surpassed this individual, their insight and guidance were an invaluable tool in getting started. Let's look at a realistic timeline for Jared to get started in full-time day trading.

Week 1: Establish my trading strategy and allocate a percentage of my portfolio to day trading. Identify the types of stocks that I want to trade and begin studying them on a daily basis. Decide if I am going to trade from home or go to a day trading firm. Try to find a mentor.

Weeks 2 and 3: Analyze the capabilities and features of a direct access trading screen. Make sure to get a clear understanding for the capabilities of each function, and start discerning which tools are going to be the most worthwhile for me to use (e.g., for news feeds). Spend an hour each day practicing my keystrokes on a keyboard.

Weeks 4 through 6: Begin simulation on a direct access trading system for half the day. Identify which areas I am going to need more time to learn. Start talking to other traders and understanding their trading rules and the information on which they base their decisions.

Week 7: Sit next to an experience trader and try to understand what makes him or her successful. (If you do not have someone to sit with, go to the next step.)

Weeks 8 through 10: Begin trading, although on a simulation device, as if it were for real. Track my trades at the end of every day, and start setting financial goals for myself.

Week 11: Go live, with the goal of losing as little money as possible every day. Be extremely conservative in all of my trades, and stick exactly to my trading strategy.

After a couple of weeks of live trading, Jared will want to go back and adjust his risk-reward profile again and update his trading strategy. If he is doing well, he may want to make the jump of trading a bit "more expensive stocks" or adding new stocks to trade to his list. If he is still having ups and downs, which is much more likely, he will want to stick with his extremely conservative style until he starts making money on a daily basis.

MAKING THE JUMP FROM LONG-TERM DIRECT ACCESS TRADING TO DAY TRADING

Still looking at the previous examples, if Joe (the long-term direct access trader) wanted to make the jump to day trading, there would be a couple of things he would need to do. First, he would have to make sure that he had the appropriate time to devote to day trading. Even if he was only going to day trade new IPOs, this still requires a commitment to be able to devote the appropriate amount of time. It could be very difficult to do this if Joe is at his full-time job in meetings every morning, for example, and cannot get back to his computer screen or if Joe really does not have time on a daily basis to review the intraday charts of the two or three stocks he thinks he wants to day trade. When you day trade, a whole new set of factors that arises. You must have the time and interest in dealing with them before you make the jump. However, once Joe has mastered the fundamentals of long-term direct access trading, he will be much better suited to identifying whether he is ready and interested in making the jump. Joe just needs to realize that when he decides to make that jump, there will be a considerable amount more required from him to be successful with it.

MAKING THE JUMP FROM PART- TO FULL-TIME DAY TRADING

Still looking at the previous examples, if Jennifer (the part-time day trader) wanted to make the jump to full-time day trading, she would need to evaluate a couple of key points. Can she afford to make the jump and potentially not have any income for 3 to 6 months? Is she having success with her part-time day trading? Does she love the intensity and action of the financial markets? These are all very important questions that need to be answered before Jennifer makes the jump. In addition, Jennifer will need to spend significantly more time broadening the number of stocks she follows. She will have to get more comfortable watching and trading multiples stocks over the course of a day. In addition, it can be very draining for new full-time day traders to become accustomed to the intensity of the trading day. Although the markets are open only from 9: 30 A.M. until 4:30 P.M. EST, trading is one of the most intense professions in the world. Jennifer should spend some time mapping out her goals and interests and make sure that it is the right decision for her. If she decides to do it, she will then need to find the right environment (home or a day trading firm) and then go for it.

QUESTIONS TO ASK YOURSELF

1   What type of direct access trader do I want to be (day trader, part-time day trader, long term)?

2   How much time am I going to be able to devote to direct access trading?

3   What risk level am I comfortable assuming?
4   What is my trading strategy going to be?
5   How frequently am I going to update my trading strategy?
6   What core group of stocks am I going to follow?
7   What are the three trading rules I will live by?

C H A P T E R

INTERPRETING REAL-TIME NEWS AND INDICATORS

One of the most important keys for success in direct access trading is knowing which real-time news and indicators you need to pay attention to. Because you are now privy to a wealth of new information, it becomes more important than ever to understand what effect specific pieces of information can have on your various long- and short-term holdings. This chapter looks at the new information available to direct access traders. Most traders are amazed by their newfound information once they become accustomed to using it and wonder how they ever traded without it. But some individuals can become "paralyzed" by the abundance of new information and need to very carefully select which pieces of information they rely on for their trading decisions so that they can more efficiently capitalize on opportunities in the marketplace. However, do not fear this new abundance of information. Even the best direct access traders in the world use only certain pieces of this infor-

mation to make their trading decisions. However, over the years, they pour over these data day after day and fine tune their understanding of this information to make better trading decisions. Selecting these pieces of information in large part depends on the trader's overall trading strategy. A day trader is going to look at a very different level of detail on a stock than a long-term direct access trader. But there are certain core pieces of information that both of them will look at when placing their trades to get in at the best price possible. Most individuals have never used such things as level II quotes when placing their trades. Every direct access trader uses different pieces of information in the market. In addition, each direct access trader interprets that information in different ways, based on his or her own research and what he or she is looking for the stock to do. There are, however, a couple of key elements that every direct access trader should take into account, and these will be discussed in the following sections.

HOW HARD IS IT?

Interpreting real-time news and indicators is no different from interpreting any other type of financial news. The only difference is that real-time news is exponentially more valuable than day-old news. The speed at which nonprofessional traders and investors can access information has increased dramatically with the power of the Internet. Once upon a time, people actually had to look in the newspaper the next day to find out how their stocks did. Although some individuals still do this, anyone can now see real-time quotes, and direct access traders can even see level II quotes. As much progress as the Internet has made in enabling individuals to receive news in a more timely fashion, only direct access traders can access the critical trading information that Wall Street professionals use. News has a very finite life span in terms of its effects on a stock. What you can do with a piece of news that is real time versus a piece of news that is 1 minute old is significant. Once the market has heard the news, whatever it is, there is usually a very finite window before the stock actually starts to move. In fact, in many cases, as with earnings reports, the stock sometimes performs its entire move based on expectations. Thus the key becomes harnessing the power of real-time news and indicators. If you are a long-term direct access trader, this may mean email alerts to your computer if a stock reaches a certain price or if news comes out on a stock. If you are a day trader, this may mean color-coding your positions on the screen so that you can quickly tell what is happening with your positions just based on color. The key to capitalizing on real-time news and indicators is being fast. Direct access trading tools provide the execution speed, but you still must digest, interpret, and harness the information before everyone else does.

TECHNICAL VERSUS FUNDAMENTAL

Direct access trading involves the right combination of technical and fundamental analysis. Each direct access trader uses a different blend of these two types of information. In the next chapter we get into both of these in a little greater detail. The key is to understand the basics of what each provides and then pick the specific things to look at over the course of a trading day. At its most basic level, *technical analysis* refers to items such as charts, graphs, formulas, and other numbers-oriented information that traders use, whereas *fundamental analysis* refers more to information such as market and stock-specific news. There is more information available in the marketplace than any one individual could ever consume over the course of a day, so it becomes imperative to focus your efforts on the most pertinent information. The following paragraphs highlight some of the most important fundamental and technical indicators to look for.

BASIC TECHNICAL INDICATORS

Basic indicators are usually things such as price and volume of shares being traded. Although these sound fairly simple, and are used by everyone, there is a plethora of ways to use these pieces of information. For example, the price of a stock is probably the most examined piece of information by every direct access trader. Traders analyze price on an intraday basis, over a month, over a year, and since a stock began trading. They look for patterns where a stock acts in a similar manner over time. They also examine how the price of a stock reacts to general market news, earnings reports, and even times of the day. The stock price is the focal point of every trader. However, each trader analyzes the stock price in a different way in order to making better trading decisions.

Level II quotes are another excellent source of information for direct access traders. Previously only for Wall Street professionals, direct access level II quotes let you actually see who is buying and selling a stock and at what prices. You actually can see the entire market for the stock on your screen and use this information to help you see the different buying and selling pressures on the stock. You will be able to see if the current bid for stock XYZ is 34 and Goldman Sachs and Morgan Stanley both have offers for 1000 shares at 34⅛. This is one example of large institutions potentially moving the price of the stock higher, meaning a good buying opportunity for you. Level II quotes are one of the best tools for direct access traders. Whether you are a day trader or long-term direct access trader, level II quotes give you the full picture of what is happening to a stock. It is like being able to see the whole picture instead of just a snapshot from a long way away. Every direct access trader should learn how to use and interpret level II quotes for all trades.

Another highly examined indicator is the number of shares traded of a particular stock. The more shares of stock traded, the greater is the liquidity for everyone trading that stock, and the better is the chance for movement within that stock. Volume patterns of a stock are a good indication of whether a stock is coming in or out of favor. If a stock is trading up on heavy volume, this is usually a good indicator that market sentiment for the stock is favorable. Many day traders use this information for intraday gains on stocks where the volume is picking up steam and the stock looks to be breaking through. Other longer-term direct access traders examine the volume of shares traded at different points during the year to try to understand when it is a good time to buy or sell a stock.

Technical analysis can only help you interpret what has happened in the past. This is the information that can be used to attempt to predict what is going to happen in the future, but there is no guarantee. However, over time, certain patterns do develop that give you a much clearer idea of where a stock is heading in the short and long term. Direct access traders always should be focusing on the historical prices and volume of shares being traded for their stocks. They can then augment these indicators with more sophisticated measures of technical analysis that they feel will help them make better trading decisions.

TRADING RANGES

Once you have analyzed a stock for any significant period of time, you can start to tell the trading ranges in which a stock trades. A *trading range* is a particular range of prices that a stock has traded in over a given period of time. It can be over a year, a month, a day, or even an hour. Depending on your direct access trading strategy, you will look at different periods of time to identify the various trading ranges for a stock. The historical pattern of a stock is your best indicator of future movements of that stock. Day traders especially look at the way a stock trades in the morning and right before the close of markets to find any clues regarding short-term movement of the stock. Longer-term direct access traders look at monthly and annual charts to determine whether a stock is due to break through in the near future, thus making it a good buying opportunity. One important thing to remember about trading ranges is that from stock to stock, trading ranges can be wildly different. For example, an Internet company that has just gone public is likely to have a much wider trading range over their first year than a traditional brick and mortar retailer that has been public for years. Also, it is important to analyze the trading ranges of comparable stocks in the same industry. If stock XYZ does the same thing as stock ABC, but the trading range of XYZ over the last year has been $46 to $60 and that of ABC has been $12 to $24, it is important to understand the differences and what will cause the gap to narrow between the two ranges. Most people incorrectly compare the prices of stocks at face value, rather than doing research on why the trading ranges are different. This can be the case because of the number of shares outstanding, because particular institutions are holding onto their shares and not trading them in the marketplace, or simply because a company has ten times the revues and profits. Regardless of what type of direct access trader you are, identifying the trading ranges of the stocks in which you are active is one of the best ways to identify good buying and selling opportunities.

IMPORTANT GROUPS AND PIECES OF NEWS

Certain pieces of fundamental news will always have an effect on every stock. General market sentiment is largely driven by general news events, many of which have nothing to do with the stock market or specific stocks within them. For example, in times of war, almost all stocks on the stock market traditionally have declined. However, it is possible for every piece of news to have some effect. The problem is that there has never been any quantifiable way to tell which pieces of news will have which effect. In many cases, breaking news can have a snowball effect, where a piece of normally insignificant news can propel a wave of action within a particular stock. Once again, the best way to know if this is going to happen to one of your stocks is to examine the way that previous news events have affected that stock. Because this can be hard to do on a historical basis, except for major news events, it is especially important for day traders and part-time day traders to monitor the daily activities of a stock to start to understand the "personality" of that particular stock. It is amazing what can be learning by monitoring the activities of a stock on a daily basis. Even if you are not making trades on a daily basis, by being in such close contact with the way a stock moves, you are well positioned to identify both a short- and long-term buying opportunity. The key is to make mental notes as to the way your stocks react to general pieces of market news, industry news, and information that affects the stock specifically. Let's take a look at some of the key fundamental news events that affect almost every stock.

The Fed

The chairman of the Federal Reserve (the Fed) is arguably the most important "bellwether" of the stock market. Television news reporters have even gone so far as to monitor the size of his brief case on days when he is announcing decisions to raise, maintain, or reduce interest rates in order to get an idea of what he is going to say. Because his comments have such an effect on the market in general, the chairman of the Federal Reserve has considerable power with respect to moving the world's financial markets. However, as is the case with most news that is expected to break at a specific point in time, most of the time stock prices have already moved based on what the majority of "experts" feel the chairman's comments are going to be. Nonetheless, some of the most active trading days are days when the Fed makes announcements. Every direct access trader should know when the Fed is making announcements and monitor the financial news sources to get an idea on what the Fed is going to do.

Inflation

The Fed makes its decision to raise, lower, or maintain interest rates based on inflation. Inflation affects our entire economy and thus can have serious effects on every stock. When inflation is low, usually the economy is "humming along," and consumers in general have more expendable income on nonstaple products and services such as entertainment and travel. However, as inflation increases, and in times of economic hardship, individuals are much less likely to be buying certain products and services. New reports come out every week that somehow tie into inflation.

Keep an eye on the big ones, such as the job report, and any others that could affect stocks you trade specifically.

Analysts' Reports

Analysts' reports are excellent indicators of where the price of a stock is heading. Research analysts release these reports, usually on a quarterly basis, identifying their price target for a particular stock, their rating of the stock, and their general thoughts. Depending on the source of the comments (obviously, the research analysts at big firms such as Goldman Sachs and Morgan Stanley Dean Witter carry much greater weight), such reports can affect stock prices considerably. These research analysts are often some of the most well-versed individuals on specific industries. On a daily basis they are in frequent contact with the leading individuals in various industries. Because companies want to be "covered" by research analysts, they are usually very open to sharing their numbers and information on where their company is heading. The thing to keep in mind about analysts' reports, especially for Internet and technology companies, is that the analysts themselves are "guessing." Although they have access to some of the best information available, there is no guarantee that their findings will hold true. For example, valuation techniques for Internet and technology companies are now entirely different from those for other types of companies. It is impossible to use traditional measures to explain why companies such as Amazon.com and Yahoo! have such high market capitalizations. Therefore, research analysts also have to find new ways to value companies using new pieces of information and creating different types of analyses.

Lawsuits

Lawsuits are another example of important information that can affect the price of a stock. Public companies are required to make public any lawsuits that are filed against them. This information can be found in a company's quarterly (10q) or annual (10k) financial statements, which can be found for free on sites such as Free Edgar (*www.freeedgar.com*). Look especially for multiple lawsuits focused around a single topic. For example, public Internet audio companies have been in the spotlight because of copyright issues with respect to MP3 files. Many have suffered a significant downfall in their price, and it remains to be seen if they will ever bounce back unless they are victorious with their cases. Another example is the tobacco companies, which face multiple class action lawsuits with respect to their products. And finally, the Microsoft antitrust trial is another excellent example of an incident that is affecting not just Microsoft stock but technology and Internet stocks in general. Regardless of whether you are making short- or longer-term trades, it is important to at least be aware of any significant lawsuits against a company in which you are interested and when potential rulings are expected to take place.

Acquisitions

Acquisitions are one of the most significant events that can affect the price of a stock. Even when a company is rumored to be "in play," often its stock price can rise significantly. This holds true frequently for an entire industry. For example, when AOL purchased Time Warner, other comparable powerhouse Internet stocks such as Yahoo! and Amazon.com were thought to be "in play" or "on the prowl." Thus their stock prices rose significantly. However, just because a company is rumored to be in the process of making or makes an acquisition does not mean that the stock prices of either one of the companies are definitely going to rise. In the case of the AOL–Time Warner merger, the AOL stock in fact went down when the deal happened, whereas the Time Warner stock went up significantly. Frequently, the reaction of the investment community, especially Wall Street analysts, sets the tone for the way a stock reacts. Direct access traders who are tuned into what is happening, however, are usually some of the first ones to be able to take advantage of the opportunity. In fact, many day traders subscribe to services that list stocks thought to be "in play" and thus that need to be watched during the course of a trading day.

Key Hires and Fires

Human capital has become the most important asset for every company, especially given the current crunch for experienced executives. When a company is able to land a key executive, especially a chief executive officer (CEO), this can signal a great buying opportunity for the company's stock. On the other hand, if a board of directors decides to fire a current CEO, this often signifies turmoil within the company. What this means for direct access traders is that it is a good idea to keep an eye peeled for formal announcements by public companies you trade with regard to new hires and fires. In fact, when a company fires or hires a key individual, such as a CEO, it is required to file an S-8 form with the Securities and Exchange Commission (SEC). However, as a direct access trader, you want to find out about this a lot sooner.

Partnerships

Key partnerships also can play an important role in a public company's stock price spiking up or down. However, do not be seduced into thinking that just because a stock you trade has reported a partnership, the price is going to go up. The term *partnership* can mean such a broad range of things that it is important to get a true understanding of what is really happening. A partnership can simply mean that companies have agreed to trade links from their Web sites, or on the other hand, it can mean that they are going to form a substantial new product line together. In addition, Wall Street often has a funny way of determining on its own whether a partnership is good or not. In fact, frequently, a partnership agreement may not be well publicized, and therefore it may have little short-term effect on a stock. It is always a good idea, however, to monitor press releases by companies in which you are interested. Look for hints in quotes from the CEO or other key individuals in the company for specific things to watch for in the future.

Similar IPOs

IPOs are one of the best bellwethers for a particular industry. Companies are always compared by their market capitalizations (number of shares outstanding $\times$ share price). Therefore, if a new company has exploded onto the scene and has amassed a market capitalization that is disproportionate to that of other companies in the space, it often makes for an interesting stock to trade. Whether the stock appears to be seriously undervalued or overvalued, there are numerous opportunities if you understand the fundamentals behind other stocks in the industry. A strong IPO by a company in a particular industry often can cause positive spikes in other similar public companies as well if analysts get "hot" about an industry. Conversely, if it looks like the new entrant is going to be eroding market share from some of the incumbent companies, the opposite can hold true as well. Regardless, IPOs are one of the best indicators for traders looking at specific industries.

War

Fortunately, war is not something that we consistently declare in the United States. However, when the United States is at war, there are definite effects on the stock market. Liquidity is what makes the stock market the efficient market that it is today. In times of war, individuals on average tend to put less money into stocks as a whole. There is an undeniable ripple effect throughout the entire market when this happens. In addition, as direct access trading tools open up new opportunities to trade securities overseas, it will become increasingly important to stay well abreast of political tension in other countries as well. Fortunately, the United States is at war a lot less often than most other countries. However, a war in another country can have a serious effect on a stock you are trading that is based in that country.

Specific Announcements by an Institution

Institutions often make announcements regarding particular stocks independent of their analysts' recommendations. For example, Goldman Sachs may announce that it has been engaged by a particular company to help explore opportunities overseas, acquire companies in the industry, or even sell the business. Although this information often finds its way out into the open before a company is ready to release it, as soon as the word hits the street, there is often a significant up or down tick in the stock price. Although this is of little interest to long-term direct access traders, it is precisely the type of information that day traders thrive on. The ability to get such information quickly means providing an opportunity for day traders to make a play on the stock.

Specific Wall Street institutions to watch for such announcements include

Goldman Sachs
Morgan Stanley Dean Witter
Salomon Smith Barney
Lehman Brothers
Credit Suisse

Although these are the big names, there are a handful of other smaller investment banks that also can have a significant effect on any given stock. This is especially the case if the company has formal ties to them, such as being the underwriter that took the company public.

Chat Rooms and Message Boards

Chat rooms are a highly debated source of information for all traders. Sites such as Raging Bull (www.ragingbull.com) and the Motley Fool (www.fool.com) have served as excellent forums for individuals to discuss their trades and specific stocks, but each piece of information needs to be taken with a grain of salt. In terms of information, on the one hand, you have the credited Wall Street analysts issuing their reports, and on the other, you have chat rooms and message boards. Although some traders have found out about new stocks this way or have found out a piece of hot information that appeared on the boards before anywhere else, be wary of everyone and everything you read. Chat rooms and message boards often serve as excellent ways to find information on stocks, but you should never take anything you read in them for granted. One of the best ways to find out about new stocks and to learn different things about stocks is from other traders. When they are right next to you, it helps because you know a little bit more about them. However, there are still valuable nuggets of information to be taken away from chat rooms and message boards. In particular, these sources are good forums for traders to gauge the "pulse" of a particular stock. Often you can sense the different emotions and ideas circulating about a stock by reading these areas. Day traders in particular try to put together the pieces of the puzzle to understand the "personality" of a specific stock, and message boards and chat rooms can be an excellent place to get some additional information. Just remember, before you act on any information you find in these areas, do your own homework to double-check the accuracy first. Most chat rooms are free, but for some, you have to register first.

Here are some examples:

www.motleyfool.com
www.marketcentral.net/chat/
www.msnbc.com
www.stockresearch.com
www.investorama.com
www.marketwatch.com
www.yahoo.com

Market News

General market news can have an effect on every stock. Whether it is the threat of war, new government legislation, or even a horrific weather event, general market news is an important indicator. It is especially important to keep an eye on industry-specific news that may affect one of your holdings. Whether a new research report on an industry in general or even comments by an analyst at a Wall Street firm, industry-specific news often has real-time effects on every stock within that industry. Many direct access traders find it particularly useful to watch television channels such as CNBC to find out about breaking market news. Others subscribe to email newsletters that provide breaking news reports on various topics. The key is understanding what effect market news can have on your holdings and establishing a system to monitor breaking market news so that you can capitalize on making trades at the best possible times.

Timing

Another important factor for direct access traders is the time of the day they make their trades. Stocks tend to be the most volatile when the market opens in the morning and 30 minutes to 1 hour before it closes in the afternoon. These times of the day can prove to be excellent trading times for all direct access traders, especially day traders. In fact, most day traders place most of their trades during these time periods because of the increased volatility and increased profit potential. New direct access traders should spend a significant amount of time analyzing the way stocks move during these time periods before trying to make trades.

Level II Quotes

Level II quotes are one of the most important tools for direct access traders—if not *the* most important. Many individuals, when they place a trade using an online broker, only see the bid and ask prices for a given stock. Although these numbers represent the parameters at which the stock is trading, there is a whole additional layer of information available that is not being shown. It is like only seeing the middle of a picture when there are lots of additional details on each side that you cannot see but which make for a more complete picture. Let's take look, for example, at a typical bid-ask quote on an online broker:

MSFT 55⅞ Bid versus 56 Ask

In this case, an individual can see that the current price to buy the stock is 55⅞, whereas the current price to sell the stock is 56. Now, usually individuals using a traditional online broker are only seeing a *static quote.* This means that the quote can be as much as 15 to 20 minutes old. Therefore, the actual price may have shifted dramatically. *Real-time quotes* help solve this problem somewhat, but there is still a wealth of information about the prices being paid to buy and sell this stock that we

Figure 4-1 Nasdaq level II screen for MSFT. (*Courtesy of Tradescape.*)

are not seeing. This is where direct access traders have a significant advantage. Let's take a look, for example, at the same bid-ask quote for MSFT using a level II quote (Figure 4-1).

Level II quotes show all the individuals buying and selling the stock. This gives direct access traders a significant edge in trading the stock because they can see the upward and downward pressure being applied by various groups. These groups may include market makers, institutions, and even other traders. By being able to see this information, you have a much better chance of getting the price you want for a stock.

For example, let's see what happened the day theglobe.com went public: Within the first day of trading, the stock appreciated over 400 percent. If you had put in a market order for the stock that morning, you would have ended up paying significantly more than you initially thought, and because the stock at one point was up over 500 percent, you may have had a very quick loss if you got in at the peak. There are a couple of reasons this could have happened. First, there was no way for you to see the buying pressure as soon as the market opened. Unless you had real-time quotes, which still only would have given you a snapshot, you would have been unable to see how quickly the stock spiked upward. In addition, by using a third party to place the trade for you, the time at which the stock was traded was in their hands. Although all brokers, both online and offline, strive to fill trades in the timeliest manner possible, there is no way to tell when your stock order will be filled. Therefore, with direct access trading tools, you would have had access to the real-time news, indicators, and execution methods to place your trades in real time, directly with another party.

For day traders, level II quotes aid in finding patterns in the buying and selling habits of institutions and market makers. This is critical information used to detect patterns and interpret the short-term movements of a stock. With proper research, it is possible to get an understanding over time of the ways certain groups react to certain market conditions, technical indicators, or even specific pieces of news. For long-term direct access traders, level II quotes provide a view of the buying and selling pressure occurring within a stock. This can be of significant value, especially if you are trading with enough shares, in allowing you to gauge your timing right to get in at the best price possible. If you see a lot of downward selling pressure on a stock and wait an extra 5 minutes to make your trade, you may end up saving hundreds or even thousands of dollars. In addition, you now have the power to make your own terms. There is no blindly placing a trade and "hoping" for the best possible price.

Stock Splits

When companies announce a stock split, it is often a very good indicator that interest in the stock has reached a level where the company wants to bring the price back to a level where more individuals can afford it. It is important to remember, however, that a stock split is nothing more than an accounting function. It is no guarantee that the stock is going to go higher or that something "new and improved" is happening at the company. However, as of late, stock splits have increased volume and interest in many stocks. Especially in Internet and technology stocks such as AOL, Amazon.com, and Yahoo!, which have split numerous times over the last couple of years, each time a split was announced the stock appreciated significantly. This is not to say that it held that level over time, but the announcement of a stock split was enough to increase enthusiasm in the stock and raise the price. It is an extremely good idea to keep an eye on stocks that look to be approaching abnormally high levels, especially levels where historically the company has announced a split.

The Long Bond

The *long bond* describes the price and yield for a 30-year Treasury bond and is one of the most important indicators that traders watch every day. Although Treasury bonds are a debt instrument, they represent one of the best ways to gauge the effect of interest rates on the market. Interest rates play a major role on investor psychology, and because they fluctuate on a daily basis, they are a great real-time indicator. The general rule of thumb is that if yields on the 30-year Treasury bond are falling, the equity markets will rally. The same is true if yields are rising, where generally equities are falling. This is a great indicator for traders to be able to determine when the tides in the market are turning, especially for their shorter-term position trades. Although you may not have experience analyzing the debt markets, the 30-year Treasury bond is the best—and easiest to use—benchmark for the state of activities within the markets.

CNBC

CNBC is one of the best places for up-to-the-minute news affecting the market. Because so many traders are glued to their screens watching this over the course of the trading day, it magnifies the effects it can have on stocks mentioned. CNBC offers a number of shows airing from 5:00 A.M. until 7:30 P.M. CNBC is extremely valuable to direct access traders because it represents one of the best places to find out about breaking news. Newspapers and other print media that publish information on a daily or weekly basis are great for your general knowledge, but they are not reliable sources on which to base trading decisions. Even with financial Web sites that report events as soon as they happen, you still have to go back to them to find out about the breaking news. With CNBC on in the background, you can hear about breaking news instantaneously and act on it. Whether you just have time to watch during lunch or you keep CNBC on all day long, each program has a unique spin on what is happening in the world's financial markets. Shows currently on CNCB include

"Today's Business: Early Edition," 5:00 to 6:00 A.M.—summary of activity for the upcoming day.

"Today's Business," 6:00 to 7:00 A.M.—summary of activity for the upcoming day, stocks to watch, international markets.

"Squawk Box," 7:00 to 10:00 A.M.—Wall Street commentary and interviews.

"Market Watch," 10:00 A.M. to 12:00 noon—current business news affecting particular stocks and the market in general.

"Power Lunch," 12:00 noon to 2:00 P.M.—interviews with business leaders, market recap for the morning, and every Monday a feature on day trading.

"Street Signs," 2:00 to 4:00 P.M.—what to look for in the closing hours of trading for the day, movers and shakers.

"Market Wrap," 4:00 to 6:00 P.M.—recap of the day's events, winners and losers, what is set to come in the days ahead.

"The Edge," 6:00 to 6:30 P.M.—focus on trends affecting business, now and in the future.

"Business Center," 6:30 to 7:30 P.M.—recap of the day.

NEWS TO IGNORE

With so much news available on every stock in the marketplace, it becomes almost as important to know what you can ignore. It is very easy to get bogged down in too much information that slows down your thought processes by making you think too much. Remember, in direct access trading the name of the game is speed. Because you now have access to the same tools as Wall Street professionals—most important, real-time executions and level II quotes—you have to take advantage of it. You have to identify the sources of information you use, the indicators you look at, the criteria a stock needs to fit before you buy or sell it, and then execute. If you are a day trader, all of this needs to happen within seconds so that you can capitalize on an opportunity immediately. If you are a long-term direct access trader, it is still important to only identify the sources of information that are relevant and provide unique views so that you do not become too bogged down. Most Wall Street firms have research departments that spend their entire days pouring through information, talking to CEOs, and assembling research reports. Take advantage of the time they spend and do not try to duplicate their efforts.

GETTING THE BEST POSSIBLE PRICE FOR A STOCK

The whole purpose of direct access trading is to get the best possible price for a stock. Therefore, identifying the real-time news and indicators to use is extremely important for every direct access trader. With direct access trading tools, you can in essence now browse through the available prices for a stock and select the one you want. There is no more blindly putting in a market order with your online broker hoping to get in under a certain price. When you see the price you are looking for, you can "hit" it immediately. As soon as you do this, you have either bought or sold the stock. There is no waiting for confirmation and no wondering what price you got in or out at. The way you get the best possible price for a stock is by understanding when it is a good buying or selling opportunity. You do this by studying previous trading ranges, the way a stock reacts to particular pieces of news, and then using real-time news and indicators to help you get in at the best time possible. Direct access trading does not guarantee that you will be a better trader or make more money, but you will have the best tools with which to work. If you are not using direct access trading tools, you are at a significant disadvantage in the market. Only by mastering the fundamentals of direct access trading do you give yourself the chance to consistently get the best possible price for all your trades.

HOW IS IT DIFFERENT?

The key to direct access trading is the access to real-time information and execution speeds that have only been available to Wall Street professionals in the past. Having access to information such as level II quotes and being able to monitor market maker movements allow a trader to get a much more complete picture of what is happening within a particular stock. Although this information may seem foreign at first, once you learn how to trade with it, you will wonder how you ever traded without it. Although not all the information you have access to as a direct access trader is different, your ability to get this information in real time makes it different. News and information are the most valuable commodities to any trader. By getting them even seconds before other individuals, let alone the general public who is not tapped into direct access trading tools, you give yourself a serious edge in the markets. This is no guarantee of success by any means, but you have the best information available at your fingertips in the timeliest manner possible to make your trading decisions. The key is making sure that you are plugged into the right news sources and that you are able to interpret the pieces of information on which you like to base your trading decisions. Remember, every direct access trader uses a different combination of real-time news and indicators. Depending on the types of stocks they trade and their risk-reward profile, they all use various sources for their research. However, all direct access traders use tools such as level II quotes specifically.

WHERE TO GO FOR REAL-TIME NEWS AND INDICATORS

Direct access traders like news sources that provide information in real time and display the information in such a way that they can navigate through it easily and digest large amounts from only one page. Because the name of the game is speed for direct access traders, those who find the information first and execute on it have a significant advantage over others. Although there are now hundreds of sites on the Internet for finding this information, there are a few that direct access traders use in particular. For example, direct access traders looking for information on the Internet look to Yahoo Finance, CBS MarketWatch, and Window-OnWallSt. On the television, direct access traders primarily look to CNBC. CNBC does an excellent job of analyzing stocks, investigating new "hot" stocks in the market, and providing condensed information. And although publications such as the *Wall Street Journal* and *Barron's* are not officially "real time," direct access traders still look at them very closely for insights into various stocks. In Abell, *Tools for the Direct Access Traders* in this series, we take a much more in-depth look at all these Web sites, channels, and publications to find out which are right for different types of traders. Here is a hit list of some of the major news sources.

Web Sites
The World Wide Web is an amazing resource for direct access traders. Web sites are constantly being created to offer new products and services to traders and prospective traders. However, as is often the case with the Internet, an endless amount of time may be wasted visiting sites that may not actually help you. This section lists several categories of Web sites that you will encounter and highlights several within each section, ex-

plaining their services and suggesting how they may be used. It will give you a good perspective on the different types of sites and services that exist and on what the differences are between sites in the same general subject area. The summaries and reviews of each site often distinguish between Web sites that are appropriate for a beginning trader and those which are best suited for direct access veterans. They also differentiate between sites that are most appropriate for long-term traders and those which are best for day traders. These summaries also will show you the anticipated audience of each site and will help you to figure out which types of sites would be most beneficial to your needs. Clearly, there are many more Web sites than those listed below. Once you have an understanding for the types of services offered, it may be worthwhile to explore beyond this list.

Market news

* *Flyonthewall (www.flyonthewall.com).* For $49.99 per month, or $39.99 per month if prepaid for a year, traders can have access to the news resources of theflyonthewall. Theflyonthewall warns would-be traders that "if you are looking for a general financial news site . . . then theflyonthewall is not for you." The Web site features frequently updated information on stock performance and organizes stocks by the number of information bites that the site posts; the "Stocks on the Fly" section alerts traders to stocks for which the site has posted two or more information bites in the last hour. The text is highly abbreviated and requires significant market knowledge to follow quickly.

  The site also has several other features for the day trader, including chat rooms, e-mail updates on stocks selected by the trader, and stock recommendations. Once traders are familiar with the market and its terms, theflyonthewall may be useful.

* *Yahoo Finance (finance.yahoo.com).* Yahoo Finance offers a general and educational approach to market information. Visitors can subscribe at no charge to check stock quotes and have access to the biggest financial stories via Reuters' links. The site features market information on most foreign countries and countless links to other Yahoo sites, ranging from taxes to banking.

  Traders who need immediate information should not use Yahoo Finance. This site is best geared toward investors who need infrequent market information or who want to check a stock price at the end of the day. It is also a good resource for those unfamiliar with the financial world. It offers many links that will allow beginners to grasp the key terms and concepts that lay at the foundation of direct access trading. As a market news source, it is less detailed and easier to understand than more technical trading sites.

- *Online Investor (www.onlineinvestor.com)*. Online Investor offers a basic approach to market information. It features general financial and company news, as well as less immediate information such as editorial columns. It also allows the visitor to customize the site and to create a personal stock portfolio to keep track of investments, all for no cost. The site is best used by long-term investors and not by day traders; it offers basic news that will not help a day trader find a market niche immediately.

- *Bloomberg News (www.bloomberg.com)*. The giant of financial news, Bloomberg.com offers a comprehensive overview of market activity and insightful articles ranging from government interaction in industry to new technologies. While the site does not have a service to track selected stocks, individual stock information may be obtained, and information on stocks with significant market activity is readily available.

   Bloomberg offers a service for all traders: It summarizes market activity on a large scale, points out general trends, and offers insight into government activity that may affect the market. It is less useful for day traders who need specific information quickly, but it is abundantly useful for those entering direct access trading who need to familiarize themselves with the basics of markets and finance.

Market research

- *Multex (www.multex.com)*. Multex is geared toward both individual and corporate investors. It allows individual investors to perform ticker searches and download both free and for-purchase research reports from such companies as J. P. Morgan and Merrill Lynch in real time. In addition, it offers discussion groups, more detailed Web pages on Internet and telecommunications companies, and hundreds of summaries of company histories.

   Reading Multex reports will not be a quick and easy task, so if you are a day trader, you will not have time to do so during trading hours. The reports are best used if you are making a serious, large investment in a single or several companies and need the background information to make an informed decision. In this case, Multex is a better resource for long-term investors.

• *IPOCentral (www.ipocentral.com).* This Hoover's site lists companies that are debuting today, as well as those which have debuted in the current week, and includes whether trading has begun and the opening price. Each company has a link that includes a description of the company, its financial information, and its contact information. More information can be obtained by signing up with Hoover's, which is free.

Learning which companies are debuting is crucial for all types of traders. For day traders, these companies often can create quick gains. For more long-term traders, information on IPOs is still crucial, because IPOs often can affect the entire market.

• *BigCharts (www.bigcharts.com).* BigCharts.com is a visual learner's solution to the endless streams of numbers and percentages. At BigCharts, visitors can view both an annual and a daily chart of a stock's performance. In addition, charts are available for the annual and daily movements of entire markets and industries. BigCharts also features a sizable news section, with topics including U.S. stocks, bonds, technology and the Internet, and regional groupings.

Regardless of whether you are a long-term trader or a day trader, charts are a useful depiction of stock and market performance. Day traders may want to visit this site to review how their individual stocks performed during the course of the trading day; using these charts may allow you to begin to recognize key patterns. Similarly, long-term traders may want to frequently bring up yearly charts to compare the present value of their holdings (see Figures 4-2 through 4-4).

• *EDGAR Online (www.edgar-online.com).* EDGAR Online is the best resource for viewing files from the SEC. Throughout the year, public companies are required to disclose the critical business, financial, and competitive details of their activities to the SEC. These files are made available on EDGAR Online almost immediately after they are filed with the SEC. Some files are viewable at no cost. Other memberships are available ranging from $9.95 to $99.95 per month and allow members to view more SEC filings.

SEC filings may contain potentially valuable information for a trader. However, the SEC is a government watchdog agency and has little interest in showing investors where market niches may lie. For this reason, SEC filings may be good for investors considering long-term investments and who are concerned about the health of a particular company (see Figures 4-5 through 4-9).

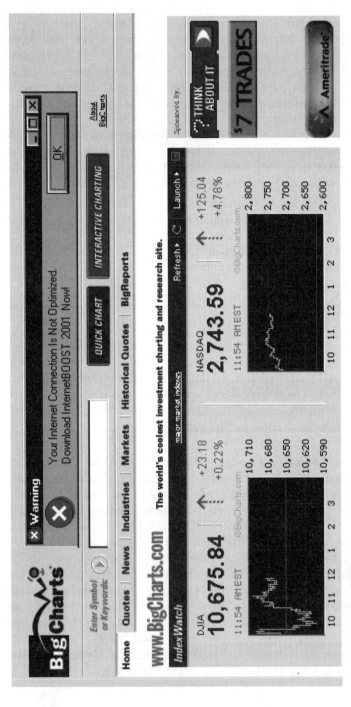

Figure 4-2 Charting a world of investment information. (*Courtesy of BigCharts, www.bigcharts.com.*)

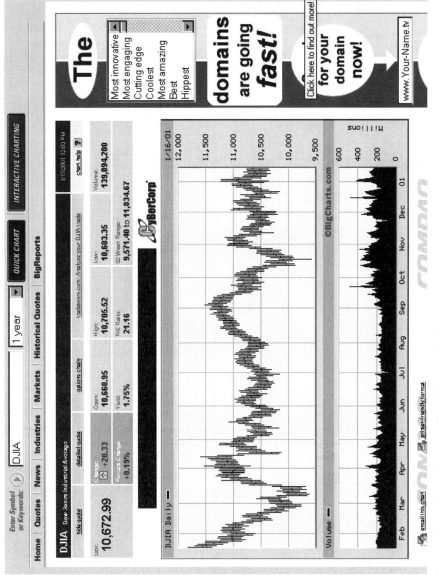

Figure 4-3 QuickCharts. (*Courtesy of BigCharts, www.bigcharts.com.*)

CMGI CMGI Inc.

1/17/2001 12:28 PM

Last:	Change:	Open:	High:	Low:	Volume:
7 13/16	▲ 1 1/8	7 17/32	7 15/16	7 1/32	13,357,000
	Percent Change: 16.82%	Yield: n/a	P/E Ratio: n/a	52 Week Range: 3.625 to 151.50	

CMGI Daily ■

1/16/01

160
140
120
100
80
60
40
20
0

@BigCharts.com

Volume ■

Millions

30
20
10
0

Feb Mar Apr May Jun Jul Aug Sep Oct Nov Dec 01

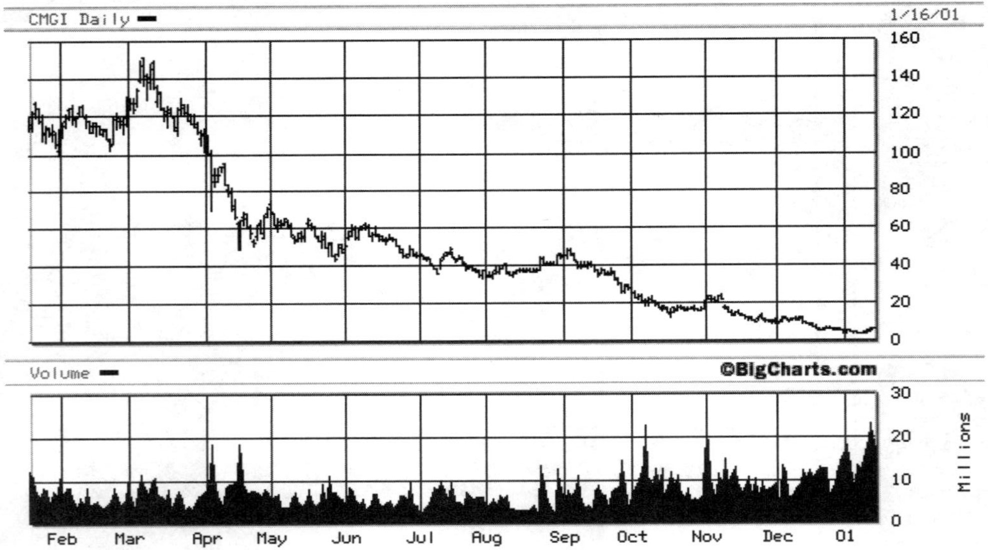

Company Data

Company Name:	CMGI Inc.
Dow Jones Industry:	Industrial Services
Exchange:	NASDAQ NM
Shares Outstanding:	319,311,000

Figure 4-4 Interactive chart for CMG Information Services, Inc. (*Courtesy of BigCharts, www.bigcharts.com.*)

EDGAR ONLINE
http://www.edgar-online.com

Home

Quick Search: [Ticker Symbol ▼] [____] [GO]

SEC Filings
- Today's Filings
- This Week's Filings
- Full Search
- Full Text Search
- People

IPO Express
- IPO Headlines
- Latest Pricings
- Upcoming Pricings
- Latest Filings

InsiderTrader

Compensation

FD-Express

Welcome to *EDGAR Online*.

Throughout the year, every U.S. public company is required to disclose the critical business, financial and competitive details of their activities to the SEC. *EDGAR Online* gives the professional and individual user fast and easy access to this SEC information. Register now for our free or subscription services.

Latest Quarterly & Annual Reports

NUOASIS RESORTS INC QUARTERLY REPORT (10QSB)

GEOGRAPHICS INC QUARTERLY REPORT (10-Q)

CASTLE HOLDING CORP ANNUAL REPORT (10KSB)

RADIANT TECHNOLOGY CORP ANNUAL REPORT (10-K)

HARRELL HOSPITALITY GROUP INC ANNUAL REPORT (10KSB)

USERNAME [____]

PASSWORD [____]

☑ Remember my username and password

[Log In]

Forgot User Name/Password
Change User Name/Password

EDGAR Online's Questions of the Day

Next Question
Source: *EDGAR Online SECrets*

Figure 4-5 The source for today's SEC filings. (*Courtesy of EDGAR Online, © EDGAR Online, Inc.*)

Figure 4-6 Latest filings. (*Courtesy of EDGAR Online, © EDGAR Online, Inc.*)

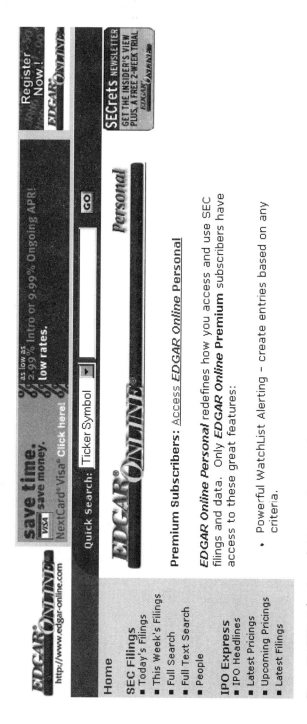

EDGAR
ONLINE
http://www.edgar-online.com

Home

SEC Filings
- Today's Filings
- This Week's Filings
- Full Search
- Full Text Search
- People

IPO Express
- IPO Headlines
- Latest Pricings
- Upcoming Pricings
- Latest Filings

save time. save money.
VISA
NextCard®Visa® Click here!

as low as
2.99% Intro or 9.99% Ongoing APR!
low rates.

Register Now!
EDGAR ONLINE

SECrets NEWSLETTER
GET THE INSIDER'S VIEW
PLUS, A FREE 2-WEEK TRIAL
EDGAR ONLINE

Quick Search: Ticker Symbol ▼   GO

EDGAR ONLINE®
Personal

Premium Subscribers: Access *EDGAR Online Personal*

EDGAR Online Personal redefines how you access and use SEC
filings and data. Only *EDGAR Online Premium* subscribers have
access to these great features:

- Powerful WatchList Alerting – create entries based on any
  criteria.

Figure 4-7 EDGAR Online Personal. (*Courtesy of EDGAR Online, © EDGAR Online, Inc.*)

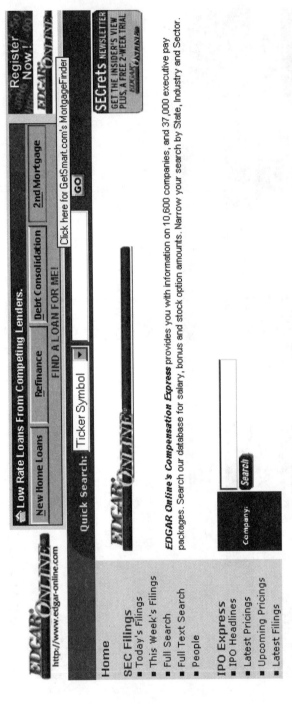

Figure 4-8 Compensation Express. (*Courtesy of EDGAR Online*, © *EDGAR Online, Inc.*)

Figure 4-9 IPO Express. *(Courtesy of EDGAR Online, © EDGAR Online, Inc.)*

Market editorial

- *Briefing.com (www.briefing.com).* Briefing.com offers three tiers of market analysis service. For no charge, visitors are allowed to view market updates and analysis every 30 minutes and also may read a series of analyst articles on current stocks. For $9.95 per month or $100.00 per year, visitors may become members of the "Stock Analysis" tier, allowing them to receive more market updates, as well as more analysis of technology stocks and IPOs. For $25.00 per month, you can have access to the "Professional" tier, which gives members everything from "Stock Analysis" to more analysis on bonds, the Federal Reserve, and several other areas.

   Briefing.com states the facts and then attempts to explain them, or predict what will happen next. Its stock ticker is a little slow (quotes are delayed by 15 minutes), but its analysis is often simple and to the point. Quite obviously, day traders will not have time to frequent this type of site. However, for those first entering online trading, reading analyses like those presented on Briefing.com will give you a sense of how people interpret movements in the markets and in stocks (see Figures 4-10 through 4-13).

- *TheStreet (www.thestreet.com).* With over 20 commentators, TheStreet.com contains a series of articles ranging from market news to company information and personal finance. The site is well designed and, perhaps best of all, is completely free. The articles are well written and read much like the articles in a normal financial newspaper. Articles range from purely factual to largely editorial. While TheStreet.com will not provide the hard-core corporate and market analysis that some traders want, it does offer interesting articles that will be useful to anyone following the market. It may be of particular use to those who engage in occasional trading but who work during most of the day because it adds another bit of news or a new article every few minutes (see Figures 4-14 through 4-18).

- *Fortune (www.fortune.com).* Fortune.com, the online version of the popular *Fortune Magazine,* is geared toward the corporate workplace. Like *Fortune Magazine,* it contains its famous lists, ranging from the "Best Companies to Work For" to the "Most Admired Companies." Fortune.com also has a strong emphasis on technology, employment, and traditional magazine-style news stories.

   Fortune.com is another site that would-be traders may want to visit to become acquainted with the terms of the trade; the site is generous enough to offer a glossary and can hardly be considered

BRIEFING.COM®

Live Market Analysis

The Perfect Companion to Online Trading™

Briefing.com is the leading Internet provider of *live* market analysis on the US stock and US fixed income markets. We provide expert commentary and analysis more frequently than any other online firm. Take a Free Trial and see for yourself.

New to Briefing.com?
Take a Free Trial!

ABOUT BRIEFING
▶ Why Briefing
▶ Awards
▶ Partners
▶ Press
▶ Testimonials
▶ FAQs
▶ Privacy Statement

FREE Realtime Quotes @ Scottrade

CONTACT US
▶ Advertising
▶ Business Dev
▶ Support
▶ Sales
▶ Feedback
▶ Editorial
▶ Directory

Free Services

Always Free

A subset of our services:

Live Market Coverage
Hourly In Play®
3x/day Up/Downgrades
Live Story Stocks®
Live Splits Calendar
Live Economic Calendar
3x/day Bond Coverage

Always Free

Stock Analysis™

$9.95 per month
Free Trial

Live analysis...
Live Stock Briefs
Live In Play®
Live Up/Downgrades
Tech Stock Analysis
Earnings Calendar
IPO Calendar
Searchable Archive

Subscribe Now

Professional™

$25.00 per month
Free Trial

Stock Analysis plus....
Live Bond Coverage
Live FX Coverage
Live Bond Briefs
Economic Analysis
15 minute Bond Quotes
Fed Policy Analysis
Yield Curve

Subscribe Now

Figure 4-10 Briefing.com home page. (*Courtesy of Briefing.com.*)

Figure 4-11 Briefing.com stock ticker. (*Courtesy of Briefing.com.*)

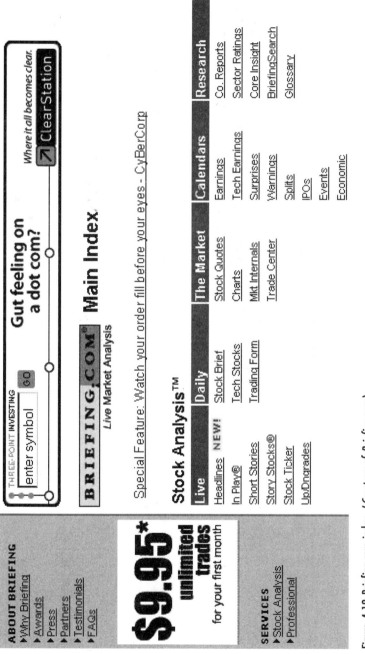

Figure 4-12 Briefing.com index. (*Courtesy of Briefing.com.*)

BRIEFING.COM® outfitted by **QUOTE.COM**

Make your own
Fortune
30 day free trial

LYC〉S BUY & SELL

Portfolio	Enter one or more ticker symbols:
Current Portfolio Quotes	[quote]
Edit Your Portfolio	If you do not know the symbol you may search for it

For general market information click here:
Intraday Charts Stock Market Indices/Forex Industry Groups

Fundamental Information provided by Market Guide
NYSE and AMEX quotes are delayed by at least 20 minutes.
All other quotes are delayed by at least 15 minutes.
© 1995-2000 Quote.com, Inc.

Figure 4-13 Briefing stock quotes. (*Courtesy of Briefing.com.*)

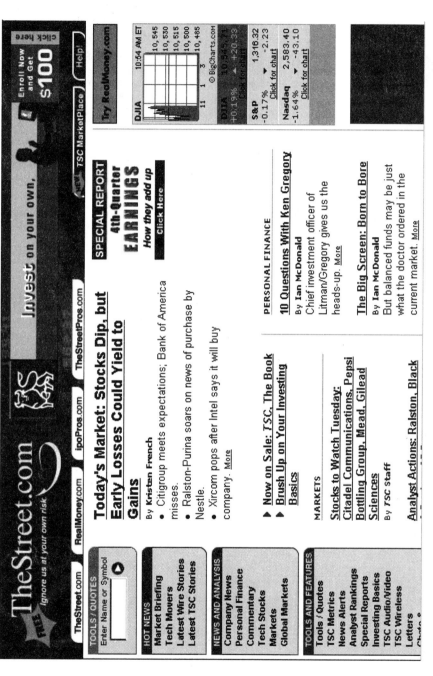

Figure 4-14 TheStreet.com home page. (*Courtesy of TheStreet.com.*)

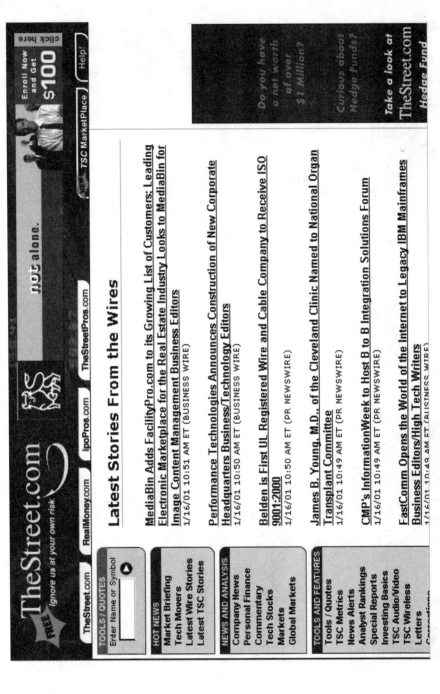

Figure 4-15 Latest stories. (*Courtesy of TheStreet.com.*)

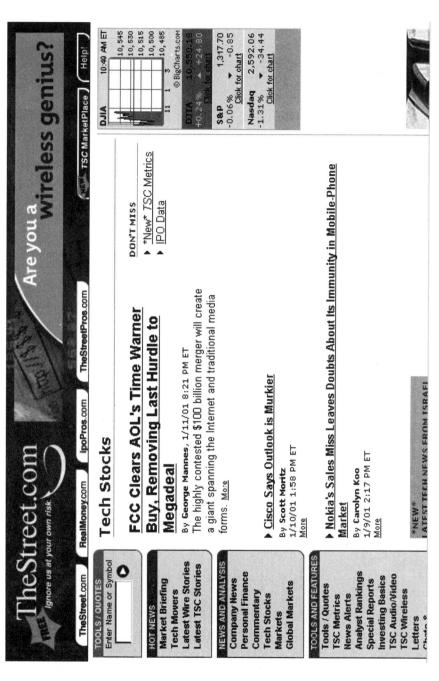

Figure 4-16 Tech report. (*Courtesy of TheStreet.com.*)

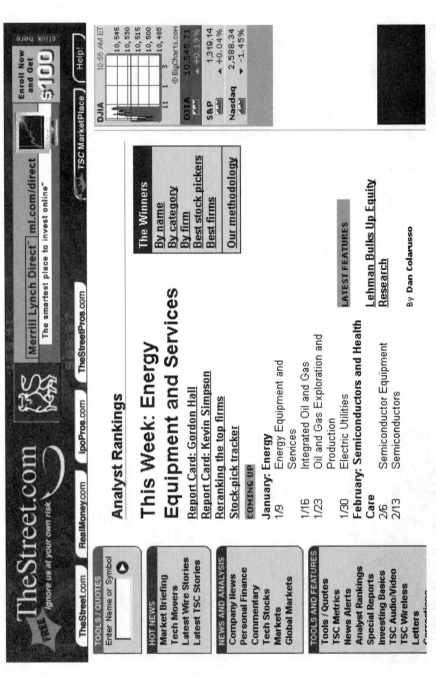

Figure 4-17 Analyst ranking index. (*Courtesy of TheStreet.com.*)

TheStreetPros.com
TheStreet.com

Subscription Checklist	**Welcome to *TheStreetPros.com***	Learn More

To register for a subscription or free trial at *TheStreetPros.com*, we request the following information:

* E-mail address and password
* Name, address and phone number
* Valid credit card

By completing the subscription process, you will be able to access *TheStreetPros.com* immediately. We will bill your credit card either monthly or annually on the anniversary of your subscription date. This is a secure site
to protect your

TheStreetPros.com cuts through the market noise to provide the most pertinent, actionable market news and commentary available for financial professionals and active traders.

- What's the action with a particular company?
- What's the story behind the story?
- What are the market-movers saying?
- Where's the market going?
- What do I need to know—now?

With TheStreetPros.com, you get all the depth, analysis and insight filtered in a quick and easy-to-digest format. And like TheStreet.com, every day brings different viewpoints and money-making perspectives that challenge you to think—and act.

Our site features up-to-the-minute articles from our professional markets newsroom, and thought-provoking contributions from the very traders, fund managers and analysts who live on the front lines of the market.

Here's what you get:

- News, analysis and commentary: Headline-driven snapshots you can use fast to make smart investment decisions.

- "Trading Track": Real-time e-journal throughout the day with the thoughts and plays

Learn More

Click here for a Free Trial

Click here to Subscribe

Figure 4-18 The StreetPros.com subscription site. (*Courtesy of TheStreet.com.*)

technical. The success of *Fortune Magazine* guarantees that Fortune.com will supply insightful and enjoyable editorials. While it would be unnecessary to visit the site more than once a day, a weekly review of its contents may help put some of the smaller market and corporate movements into perspective.

- *Forbes (www.forbes.com).* Forbes.com is also a mirror of its popular print version, *Forbes Magazine.* Offering a wide range of feature articles, Forbes.com provides articles that, while not very indepth, provide a basic overview of their subjects, of which it covers a very large range. Unlike other media-magazine sites, Forbes does offer more stock information than usual, including a surprising amount of data from the day's market. And of course, in typical Forbes fashion, it includes the lists of the wealthiest Americans and other less than pertinent information that is still somehow enjoyable to read. While it will not help you make the best trades in a given day, it will entertain you.

Trading strategy

- *TradingMarkets.com (www.tradingmarkets.com).* Founded by professional stocks, futures, and options traders, TradingMarkets.com is a site dedicated to educating both prospective traders and those who already engage in online trading. Boasting over 10,000 paid members, the site features online trading lessons given by professional traders. Topics range from how to begin trading to the more technical intricacies of specific types of trades. The site also features commentary, stock quotes, and alerts.

  TradingMarkets.com offers a "Premium Membership" and a "Professional Trader's Membership"; both allow entrance into the online classes that are the staple of the site. A "Premium Membership" costs $12 per month, or $120 per year, whereas a "Professional Trader's Membership" costs $30 per month, or $300 per year, or if you know that you will be trading for a while, $995 per lifetime.

  Online trading, particularly given its risks, is not something that should be entered without some education. If you do not have access to people who can show you the ropes, TradingMarkets.com is a good alternative. Moreover, if you already trade but are thinking about branching out into new trades or markets, TradingMarkets.com may have what you are looking for (see Figures 4-19 through 4-23).

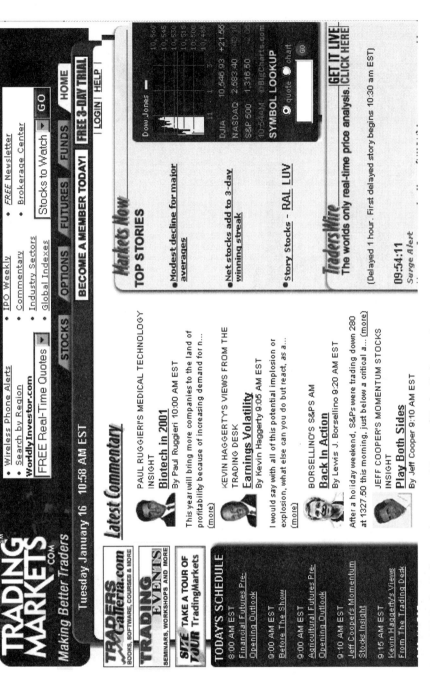

Figure 4-19 TradingMarkets.com home page. *(Courtesy of TradingMarkets.com.)*

91

Figure 4-20 TradingMarkets.com stock commentary. (*Courtesy of TradingMarkets.com.*)

Figure 4-21 TradingMarkets.com news and alerts. (*Courtesy of TradingMarkets.com.*)

Figure 4-22 TradingMarkets.com futures education. (*Courtesy of TradingMarkets.com.*)

94

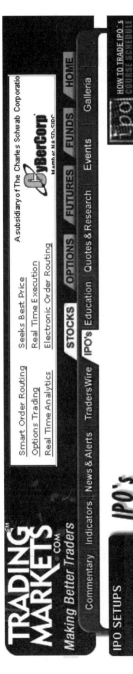

TRADING MARKETS.COM

Making Better Traders

Commentary | Indicators | News & Alerts | TradersWire | **IPO's** | Education | Quotes & Research | Events | Galleria

STOCKS | OPTIONS | FUTURES | FUNDS | HOME

Smart Order Routing	Seeks Best Price	A subsidiary of The Charles Schwab Corporation
Options Trading	Real Time Execution	
Real Time Analytics	Electronic Order Routing	CyBerCorp — Member NASD•SIPC

IPO's

IPO SETUPS

IPO SETUPS

Hot IPO Pullbacks
First-Stage Bases
Shorting-The-Hype

SEARCH [   ] [GO]

☐ Confine to this section

Now Available!
TRADERS Galleria.com

Hot IPO Pullbacks *NEW FEATURE!*

The Hot IPO Pullback is a momentum-continuation pattern used to time entries for short-term trades. A new issue will trade more than 15% above its offering price. The pattern occurs when the stock undergoes its first two-to-four-day pullback. The buy signal occurs if the stock rises 1/16 point above the prior day's intraday high.

First-Stage Bases *NEW FEATURE!*

A first-stage base is a correction-recovery pattern used to time intermediate-term trades. A new issue qualifies as a potential first-stage if it corrects from its all-time high, bottoms and then recovers at least half of the point loss incurred in the correction.

Shorting-The-Hype *NEW FEATURE!*

The Shorting-the-Hype setup is used to sell short new issues. Stocks meet the profile rose after the offering and, 30 days or later, break below the offering price where they should be shorted.

HOW TO TRADE IPO's COURSE SCHEDULE

Loren Fleckenstein's
5 Week Course:
How To Trade Hot
IPO's

TradingMarkets Stocks Editor Loren Fleckenstein teaches you the essential facts that traders need to know about IPOs. Then he teaches you three powerful setups for trading new issues. Loren also shows you how to get the most out of TradingMarkets IPO Indicators (Setups), a daily listing of new issues that may be tradable using the setups in the course.

PART 1: IPO Knowledge - In the first week of the course, I will go over everything you need to know to completely understand the IPO markets. I will show you how to identify hot IPOs, how to receive stock

Figure 4-23 TradingMarkets.com stocks: IPOs. (*Courtesy of TradingMarkets.com.*)

*   *TheHardRightEdge (www.thehardrightedge.com).* TheHardRight-
    Edge is focused on trading tactics and education. Much of this site
    is free; visitors can view "Cheetah's Radar" to learn about fast-
    moving stocks, can go to "The Trader's Wheel" to see how-to trad-
    ing strategies, and can visit "The Wizard's Den" to read strategy
    written by professional traders. The HardRightEdge also offers an
    online course that can be taken at any time of the day, has a graded
    final examination, and includes the option of a 2-hour audio lecture.
    Every student also has an online personal mentor. For $99.95,
    members receive 60 days of access to all course materials, lectures,
    and mentoring. For $119.95, the audiotape of the online lectures is
    included, and for $159.95, members can get access to all course
    materials, including the audiotape, for 6 months.

    The free strategies offered by TheHardRightEdge are a good
    place for beginning traders to start. The strategies are described in
    a how-to manner and are very easy to understand.

Community

*   *SiliconInvestor (www.siliconinvestor.com).* SiliconInvestor offers a
    wide range of trading services, most notably a wide array of chat
    rooms. Sorted by industry or type of asset, traders can ask each
    other questions, alert each other about swings in a particular stock,
    or ask questions about trading strategy. There are other more infor-
    mal chat rooms, such as "Coffee Shop," which are set up for trad-
    ers to talk politics or to meet new friends. Beyond these communi-
    cation services, SiliconInvestor also offers real-time stock quotes,
    articles, and basic strategy. Visitors also can customize their own
    portfolios and customize the site itself. To customize the site or en-
    ter the chat areas, visitors must first register, but registration is free.

    Particularly if you are trading out of your home, a site like
    SiliconInvestor that allows you to communicate with other traders
    can be invaluable. By talking to other people, you may be alerted
    to changes in stocks that you did not recognize. This could save
    you from major losses or give you a good clue to making extra
    money.

*   *Raging Bull (www.ragingbull.com).* Raging Bull acts as a forum for
    direct access traders, providing a series of chat rooms to discuss
    stocks, ask questions, and receive advice. While an occasional post-
    ing may have nothing to do with trading, most are very appropriate;
    those who register with the site have little interest in wasting time.
    Registration is free. Those who register also may create their own

Welcome to SI

LOGIN | REGISTER FREE
PRIVACY POLICY

login trading center stocktalk market tools market insight customize portfolio register FREE

Smart investors gather here™

Enter company name or symbol Symbol lookup

[   ] Search

● Quote ● Real-Time Quotes FREE
● Messages ● Web

STREAMING REAL-TIME PORTFOLIO

SIGN UP HERE   OPEN MY PORTFOLIO

Portfolio   Edit

Dow	10,634.26	-152.49	-1.4%
Nasdaq	2,291.91	-178.61	-7.2%
S&P 500	1,282.77	-37.51	-2.8%
30-yr Bond	5.24%	-0.11	
INSP	7 11/16	-1 3/12	-13.1%

WELCOME TO SILICON INVESTOR

Welcome to Silicon Investor, the foremost destination for quality investment research, editorial and community message boards.

TODAY'S COOL POSTS

[Today's Cool Posts]

- Five "will not" predictions.
- 2001 replay of 2000.
- New Year portfolio adjustments.
- Compaq's price versus growth looks good.
- I am Mr. Market maker and I own you.

TOP NEWS   Sponsored by TechStock Investor

provided by Reuters (Jan 2 3:47 pm ET)

- Stocks Fall Amid Earnings Worries
- Ford Adds Tires to Vehicle Warranty Coverage
- GE Shares Fall 8 Percent on Engine Report

What's New at SiliconInvestor

Figure 4-24. Stock talk. *(Used with permission of Go2Net, Inc.; all rights reserved.)*

97

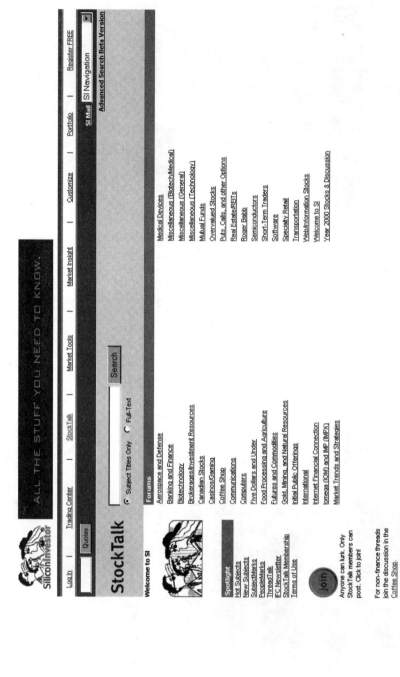

Figure 4-25. Message board directory. (*Courtesy of Investorama.com, www.investorama.com.*)

Get the IPO Calendar.

RED HERRING
BUSINESS NOW

Log In | Trading Center | StockTalk | Market Tools | Market Insight | Customize | Portfolio | Register FREE

[Quotes]

SI Mail | SI Navigation ▸

Market Tools Menu

Market Tools

Market Monitor
Delivers a quick snapshot of key indices and indicators.

Bond Market SnapShot
Offers key bond pricing and yield curve.

Annual Reports
Free annual reports for over 4,000 companies in North America and Europe.

Up/Downgrades
Provides recent changes to key analyst opinions.

IPOs
Updates you on recent filings, pricings and after-market reports.

Movers & Shakers
Shows you what's hot and what's not.

Reuters Top News
Informs you with the latest financial, political, sports and entertainment news, and more.

Figure 4-26. Market Tools menu. *(Used with permission of Go2Net, Inc.; all rights reserved.)*

chat room free of charge. This can be an especially valuable tool because it allows traders to set the agenda for a chat room and receive the type of postings that will most help or interest them. Customizing the subject area of communication can allow traders to find others who may be trading a similar stock or who may have similar questions. If you are not trading in a firm where other traders are readily available, this type of interaction may be well worth the free registration.

In addition to online communication, the site features real-time stock quotes, SEC filings from EDGAR, articles, editorials, and a comprehensive new "IPO Center." In addition, members are allowed to create their own portfolio.

- *DayTrading (www.daytrading.com).* The same site as *www.traders edge.net*, this site helps to educate traders through online communication. The site features weekly chat sessions at 5:00 P.M. EST led by a professional trader. Topics of conversation are restricted to questions that are submitted during the week prior to the chat session, allowing the chat leader to make sure that the subjects covered are both informative and popular. This also allows participants to ensure that the chat will pertain to questions they have and reduces the frivolous postings that occasionally are found on other sites with chat rooms. This type of chat session may be valuable to traders who are very new to trading and who may be confused by the technical nature of many postings on other sites. In addition, because the chats take place outside of trading hours, they will not alert traders to immediate possibilities for making money; rather, they will answer more general questions and discuss more general strategy.

  The site also features an entire section devoted to the risky elements of online direct access trading. For those who have not yet reviewed the potential risks, this section may be worthwhile. The site makes money through its own online store, which features seminars, books, and instructional tapes.

Industry resources

- *NasdaqNews.com (www.nasdaqnews.com).* Nasdaq, or the National Association of Securities Dealers Automated Quotation system, is an informative site that explains the Nasdaq and alerts visitors to Nasdaq news. The site contains a large amount of historical and statistical data on the Nasdaq Stock Market and Nasdaq indexes since their inception. There are also sections that explain the history of the Nasdaq and how it works, including the role of market makers, the kind of technology that operates the Nasdaq, and how the Nasdaq has evolved over time. There is also a comprehensive listing of IPOs since 1997 and a constant stream of Nasdaq-related news.

Understanding the history and role of the Nasdaq is necessary to give new traders a perspective on how the industry has changed and what has allowed it develop. Nasdaqnews.com provides a brief yet informative answer to such questions and familiarizes would-be traders with the Nasdaq. While the news about changes in the organizational structure of the Nasdaq may be less pertinent, like the rest of the site, it serves to show how the Nasdaq functions and how its operation affect the investments of traders.

- *NASD Regulation (www.nasdr.com)*. If you are worried that others may infringe on your finances while you trade, a visit to the NASD Web site may be worthwhile. The NASD is the independent subsidiary of the National Association of Securities Dealers, Inc., charged with regulating the securities industry and the Nasdaq Stock Market. It conducts investigations into malpractice among firms and individuals. The Web site allows visitors to file formal complaints and explains the process used to investigate potential wrongdoing. It also lists resources that best explain the rules of financial behavior. While traders hopefully will never need to use the services this site provides, it is still a good idea to know the rules that govern the actions of the parties with whom you trade. The site lists a series of contacts in the event that such a complaint is necessary.

  While it may seem that this site is unnecessary, the statistics on the site suggest that wrongdoing may be more problematic than one would assume. For example, in 1999, over 6000 formal complaints were received, 287 individuals and 4 firms were suspended, and 456 individuals were barred completely. While the percentage of offenses is still very low, these numbers show that such problems do exist. The NASD Web site is a helpful tool in the event that you experience problems.

- *New York Stock Exchange (www.nyse.com)*. The home page of the New York Stock Exchange (NYSE) is another fabulous resource for beginners. The site takes visitors through the history of the NYSE and its inner workings. Data on the NYSE are plentiful, and visitors can download the annual NYSE fact book for free. The site also features a section on regulation of the stock market, explaining the rules that govern companies and traders on the NYSE. Visitors also can view all companies currently listed with the NYSE and find out how companies get listed. There is also an educational section that details recommended books and showcases the interactive education and outreach programs that the NYSE offers.

While this site will seem very remedial to anyone who has been trading for even a few weeks, it may be helpful to people who are just starting and who do not have a clear grasp of how the NYSE works. Specifically, it may shed more light on how companies within the bounds of the NYSE operate and what types of rules govern their actions. The site is easy to navigate and does not take much time to view.

Directories

*   *InvestorLinks (www.investorlinks.com).* The best feature of InvestorLinks is its directory of Web sites. The site has links to thousands of other Web sites, organized under subject headings. InvestorLinks is solely devoted to financial Web sites and will offer a more comprehensive set of links than most mainstream search engines. It also provides brief summaries of the contents of each listed site, a great feature that will prevent you from searching through hundreds of Web sites. Companies and individuals are able to add their pages to the site. Corporate Web sites are listed in a separate directory.

    Beyond this directory, InvestorLinks also features a wide variety of news, analysis, and editorials. It also features a substantial section of charts and several weekly reports.

QUESTIONS TO ASK YOURSELF

1   Am I going to focus on fundamental analysis, technical analysis, or a combination thereof?

2   What are the different news sources I am the most comfortable understanding?

3   What particular pieces of news am I going to be looking for on the stocks I trade?

4   How am I going to make sure that I have access to real-time news and indicators?

5   What will I need to spend the most time learning in order to understand how to use this particular information?

6   How important is it that I receive breaking news in real time? How will I go about receiving it?

7   What am I using real-time news and indicators for?

5

BASIC ANALYSIS

Every trader employs some level of basic analysis when trading. How-
ever, because there are so many different types of basic analysis, it is
important that you identify the factors that are the most relevant to
your trading style. This chapter scratches the surface of the basic types
of analysis that traders of every level use. If you are unfamiliar with
any of the techniques used and want to incorporate them into your basic
analysis, you should do additional research.

Entire books have been devoted to these various types of analysis.
The key to remember is that every trader uses a different combination of
these methods. However, you need to come up with a combination with
which you are comfortable and which provides you with the right amount
of analysis to make informed trading decisions. Finding the right balance
of information is a constant struggle for all traders. You do not want to

be overloaded with information because it will prevent you from executing your trades in a timely manner. On the other hand, you need the right amount of information in order to make a well-informed and well-timed trade. The next few pages will take you through the various types of basic analysis that direct access traders use.

FUNDAMENTAL VERSUS TECHNICAL ANALYSIS

Fundamental analysis is used more for longer-term investing, whereas technical analysis is used for shorter-term trading. Fundamental analysis examines a stock's income, price-to-earnings (P/E) ratio, debt, management, industry, and a number of other aspects. It tries to take all these aspects into account to determine what the price per share "should" be. Although this sounds like the most logical way to examine a stock, numerous other factors enter the picture to cloud the situation. Nothing ever works out exactly according to plan, and the same can be said for why fundamental analysis is not perfect in identifying all the movements of a stock. There are too many tangential events happening in the world that may not have a direct effect on a particular stock but will nonetheless affect it in some way. Therefore, technical analysis helps you to more accurately analyze the shorter-term movements within a stock. Technical analysis is based on the fact that price and volume dictate the state of the market. Technical analysis uses charts to identify these patterns and make better short-term trading decisions. Everyone can see something different in a chart. However, by spending enough time analyzing charts, you can start to pick up patterns that provide clues to where a stock is going in the short term.

The three things that direct access traders using technical analysis should look at the most are volume, volatility, and momentum. These three factors are what affect a stock the most in the short term. Although it takes some practice understanding and using charts, they are an incredibly powerful tool that all direct access traders should use to get the best price possible for every stock they buy or sell. Since one of the major advantages direct access traders have over other individuals is execution speed, we will take a close look at how direct access traders can use technical analysis to gain an edge and get in at the best price possible.

Volume

Volume is what ultimately confirms the strength or weakness of trends and is the most important technical indicator for a direct access trader.

Volume levels indicate the amount of interest there is in a stock and ultimately determines the liquidity of the stock. When you see the volume of a stock picking up, this often means that interest in the stock is picking up and it is going to move (either up or down). Once the volume starts to decrease, this signifies a lack of confidence in the way the stock is now moving. Volume is the best indicator of where and if a stock is going to move. It is not necessarily an amount of volume that you are looking for but rather a significant change in volume compared with the normal level for the stock. By watching the volume levels of particular stocks over time, you get a better idea of what *significant* volume changes are.

Watching the volume of particular stocks is also a great way to find out about new and exciting stocks that might be worth trading. There is no better validation of interest in a stock than the amount of shares being traded. Therefore, keeping an eye on the most active lists for any given day is a great way to find our about up and coming stocks. On the other hand, if you see that the volume of one of your stocks has been dropping consistently over a period of time, it may make sense to replace that stock with another.

Stocks that have very little volume represent much riskier stocks to own because you may end up having a more difficult time selling them. On the other hand, stocks that have the greatest volume can be just as risky because the price can fluctuate much more quickly. If you are a direct access trader, you will want to find stocks that have enough volume that they are highly tradable, yet the amount of volume corresponds with the level of risk with which you are comfortable in the market. Day traders in particular, who feed off intraday movements of a stock, need volume and volatility to make money. Therefore, a low-volume stock is not the best place to make money. Although it is a good idea to start off in stocks that do not have the most volume, volatility is key for all day traders. The bottom line is the more volume in a stock, the more volatility it has, and the more opportunities there are to make money.

Volatility

Each direct access trader needs to find the level of market volatility with which he or she is comfortable. Each stock has its own level of volatility, and thus each stock attracts a different type of investor. Day traders prefer stocks that have the right level of volatility. A stock that has a $2 trading range over the course of a week is not a good stock for a day trader to make any money on. On the other hand, a stock that trades in the $50 trading range over the course of a week is generally too volatile and represents too much of a risk for a day trader.

Therefore, key is to find the stocks that have the right level of volatility for your risk-reward profile. If you are a long-term direct access trader, the point is somewhat moot. You want to pick stocks that you think will be the most valuable over the long term, regardless of price. If you are a day trader, you want to pick stocks that have the right level of volatility, regardless of what they do. This once again gets back to the classic difference between fundamental analysis (for long-term stocks) and technical analysis (for short-term trades). For long-term traders, it is better to own fewer shares of a more expensive stock if that stock is going to be more valuable in the long run than a less expensive stock. For day traders, it is more important to trade stocks in which you can afford to purchase more shares so as to leverage your buying power. At the end of the day, volatility is important to everyone, especially because everyone is in the markets to make money.

It is a good idea to review a stock's charts for the last month or two to get an idea of its volatility. By reviewing these charts, you will be able to see the weekly averages and pick up on any trends for the stock. Especially look at the way volume, volatility, and price interact with each other. These are the sorts of trends you try to get an understanding for so that you can use this knowledge later on when you see a similar situation. Another way to find the stocks with the right level of volatility is to look at stocks that changed significantly (up or down by more than 15 percent of their price) on the previous day. These stocks are often "in play" and represent a great opportunity for direct access traders who are comfortable with the higher level of volatility.

Momentum
The momentum of a stock is the combination of volume and volatility that keeps the price moving in the same direction. A lot of day traders are termed *momentum traders* because in all their trades they look to get in when a stock starts to make its move and ride the momentum to make a profit. Although this is just one approach to day trading, it is a highly successful method for individuals who can accurately interpret the beginning and end of a move caused by momentum. Identifying the momentum within a stock takes careful analysis of the volume and volatility levels. Individuals who have the most success with momentum trading are usually those who have the most experience within a particular stock.

Other Important Indicators for Analysis

The price per share for any given stock is another important indicator that should be analyzed. Stocks that trade above $50 a share generally are more volatile than those which trade below this amount. The same can be said for stocks that trade above $100 a share. Although many stocks split once they get to a certain price range, it is a good rule of thumb that the higher the price of a stock, the more volatile the price is going to be. You obviously also need to take into consideration the type of industry and the historical price levels of a particular stock in order to assess how volatile the stock can be.

CHARTS

Charts are one of the trader's best friends in anticipating short-term future movements of stocks. There are hundreds of different types of charts and graphs you can plot to try to interpret a stock's movement. In fact, a later book in this series is devoted entirely to different forms of technical analysis, primarily charts and graphs. Charts can only tell us about what a stock has done in the past. Using this information, we can try to understand the ways in which a stock may act in the future. Although there is no guarantee, this is one of the best "clues" for direct access traders to use in anticipating future price movements. Basically, charts are just a series of lines that go up and down and are reflective of such things as price, volume, and other indicators. By identifying patterns within a stock, you can draw trend lines that can help you to anticipate future short-term movements. The next few pages go over some of the basic forms of analysis with respect to charts.

Support and Resistance Lines

Support and resistance lines are one of the most popular forms of analysis. They help traders to understand when a stock has reached its bottom, i.e., *support,* or when it is breaking through to a new price level, i.e., *resistance.* Support and resistance lines are apparent on intraday charts as well as on multiyear ones. Stock prices obviously rise and fall over the course of a day, so it is relatively easy to determine the trading range of a stock.

Let's take a look at an extremely simple example of possible support and resistance levels for stock ABC. Stock ABC opens the day at $54 and moves up a little bit but mostly moves down over the first few hours, never breaking below $52, however. The next time the stock hovers around the $52 range may be a good opportunity because it appears at this point in time that the support level is $52. The odds are in your favor that the stock will not dip below this point, at this point in time, and will rise back up. Remember, however, that depending on whether you are making a long- or a short-term trade, your expectations on how long to hold the stock should follow accordingly. If you are looking at a 3-hour chart for ABC, you should be looking to hold it no longer than that. The same can be said if you are looking at a 3-month chart, although a lot more can happen over 3 months to disrupt the support and resistance lines (these items are discussed in the next chapter). Therefore, it is important when using support and resistance lines to understand their "shelf life" in terms of having valuable information.

It is also important to be able to identify when a stock has broken through its support or resistance levels. Your trading strategy should be in place so that you know whether to sell immediately or hold onto a stock until it dips or reaches a certain level. Also keep in mind that the amount of time and number of times that a trend line has held is the best indicator of how strong the support or resistance level is. Day traders are more concerned with the intraday trend lines, whereas longer-term direct access traders should be more interested in looking at longer-term trend lines to identify the right time to get in at the best price possible. Every trader uses technical indicators such as support and resistance lines on some level.

Reversals

Remember that although support and resistance lines may hold true for a certain period of time, there are always going to be reversals. Therefore, the key becomes identifying when a reversal is taking place and having a strategy in place if you own a stock that is trading outside its range. If the stock spikes up, then this is a good problem to have, but if the stock starts to fall, it may be time to think about selling. Frequently, when a resistance level has been overcome, it can become the support level for the next higher trading range. The same can be said of support levels, which can become resistance levels for future fluctuations in price. It is also important to remember that the convergence of trend lines can mean the end of momentum in a particular direction. This happens, for example, when a support level remains fairly constant and the resistance level begins to move toward it. This indicates that the price may drop quickly because there are fewer buyers in the market.

Chart Patterns

Two types of patterns generally are found on charts. *Consolidation patterns* occur when a stock trades in a particular range over a period of time and has multiple established upper and lower trend lines. This often means that there is a discrepancy in the market, and the price is settling into a range based on different views of where the stock price is heading. One of the best ways to tell which range the stock is going to settle into is by watching the volume levels very closely. Consolidation patterns have names such as *flags, triangles, pennants,* and *rectangles.* Rectangles, for example, get their names from the fact that when both the support and resistance lines within a stock are horizontal, the trend forms the shape of a rectangle. The other patterns get their names as well from the shapes they form when you plot the trend lines on the chart.

The other major chart pattern is a *reversal indicator.* Reversal indicators occur when a stock has traded in a particular range for a period of time and indicators start to show that the range may be changing. Names of reversal indicators include *gaps, head and shoulders,* and *double bottoms/tops.* Romeu, *Understanding Direct Access Trading* explores these topics in much greater detail.

The Psychology of Technical Analysis and Charts

Remember that hundreds, if not thousands, of other traders are viewing the same charts as you. Therefore, it is important to employ basic analysis such as support and resistance lines so that you know what the rest of the market is thinking for a given stock. Although there is never a 100 percent consensus on interpreting any chart, basic analysis is used by every trader and is your best way to gain clues about the future price movements of a given stock. Remember, if a thousand other traders see a stock not breaking through a support level, this is a great indicator that buying pressure may mount and move the stock higher.

MARKET MAKER MOVEMENTS

One of the basic forms of analysis that every direct access trader should (try to) understand is market maker movements. *Market makers* are National Association of Securities Dealers (NASD) member firms that use their own capital to represent a stock and compete for customer orders. Market makers are a significant force in every stock and are one of the best sources of information for direct access traders. There are over 500 market makers. The main ones are

BEST	Bear, Stearns & Co., Inc.
BTAB	Alex, Brown & Sons, Inc.
GSCO	Goldman, Sachs & Co.
HMQT	Hambrecht & Quist, LLC
HRZG	Herzog, Heine, Geduld, Inc.
JANY	Janney Montgomery Scott, Inc.
LEHM	Lehman Brothers, Inc.
MADF	Bernard L. Madoff
MASH	Mayer and Schweitzer, Inc.
MLCO	Merrill Lynch, Pierce, Fenner & Smith, Inc.
MOKE	Morgan, Keehan & Co., Inc.
MONT	Nationsbanc Montgomery Securities, LLC
MSCO	Morgan Stanley & Co., Inc.
NITE	Knight Securities, L.P.
OLDE	Olde Discount Corporation
OPCO	CIBC Oppenheimer Corporation
PIPR	Piper Jaffray, Inc.
PRUS	Prudential Securities, Inc.
PWJC	Paine Webber, Inc.
RAJA	Raymond James & Associates, Inc.
SBSH	Smith Barney, Inc.
SHRP	Sharpe Capital, Inc.
SHWD	Sherwood Securities Corporation

The key is to be able to identify market markers within a particular stock you are trading and try to form an understanding about their movements in the market. Although it takes time to understand market maker movements, over time this can be one of the best forms of analysis for all direct access traders.

SPECIFIC METHODS OF ANALYSIS

There are two types of basic analysis that can be used to determine a stock's price and its movement. The first is *fundamental analysis*. This type of analysis examines the fundamentals of a company—its price-to-earnings (P/E) ratio, future earnings potential, dividends, income, debt, management, market share, etc. Fundamental analysis strives to determine where a share price *should* be, based on a company's current characteristics and future potential. Fundamental analysts attempt to identify reasons that a company is or *should be* successful.

This analytical model is designed for those interested in long-term investing. It holds very little for day traders. As a day trader, you are concerned with where a share price will be in the coming minutes and possibly hours. Where a company will be in the coming weeks, months, and years—its future potential—is really of no concern to you. You are looking only at the very short term, and you are concerned only with the movement of price. However, if you are a longer-term direct access trader, you need to take all these things into consideration.

Some fundamentalists actually believe that the market is so efficient that all news and information about a specific stock are instantaneously reflected in its price. Thus they assert that technical analysis is useless. Day traders believe that many of the fundamental, technical, and psychological factors that relate to a specific company do experience a lag time before being reflected in the company's stock price. They must. If there were no lag time, there would be no day trading. You would never have the chance to be ahead of the other market participants. And being one step ahead, anticipating price changes, is how you make your money as any type of trader. Your goal is to already be there when the rest of the market participants buy and cause the price to move in your favor.

When examining stock price in the short term, technical analysis is key in making investment decisions. It allows you to use simple charts and graphs to see where a company will be *today*. It is the most dynamic trading discipline there is, and you have to work hard to use it to your advantage. Once you become adept at this type of analysis, though, you will quickly recognize patterns that you think are likely to repeat themselves. Technical analysis is based on acceptance of the fact that past patterns will repeat.

In fact, technical analysis is significantly based in psychology. You are poring over your charts and graphs not to determine how well a company is managed or what its future earnings potential might be but rather to determine how likely it is that hundreds of other traders looking at the same charts and graphs at the same time will be drawing the same conclusions you are. If enough traders see the same pattern in the charts and graphs, chances are they will react in the same manner, either buying or selling stock. Thus the pattern will be reliable enough for you to trade successfully. Basically, the psychology of the market is reflected in these charts and graphs. The charts and graphs reveal price patterns, and price patterns reflect human behavior. Let's put it this way: Even if technical analysis is a complete crock, it is so widely followed by traders that it becomes a self-fulfilling prophecy.

As a trader, your aim is to come to your conclusions just a little ahead of the market. You want to buy in before the crowd and ride a trend to profits. People control the markets and react to them in ways that can be recognized, measured, and predicted—*psychology.*

Technical analysis is certainly not the "be all" and "end all" of direct access trading. It is certainly not a sure-fire method that will tell you all you need to know to make a fortune as a day trader. There is no such method. Successful trading is a conglomeration of many methods of analyses, types of information, hunches, etc. However, technical analysis does help you to generate ideas and determine entry and exit points. It makes trading a little safer because it takes some of the emotion out of your trading decisions. It keeps you disciplined and sets boundaries. Technical indicators remind you to exit trades before you get greedy. They should be like bells going off in your head as your emotional side is getting swept away in the exciting tide of the trade.

Which types of stocks have been analyzed technically with the greatest success? The answer is stocks in the technology sector of Nasdaq. Why? Because this sector has been so active and has produced so much data. It is more ripe for analysis than other sectors. Most seasoned traders recommend that you trade these stocks over 1- to 5-day periods. There are many technical indicators for you to examine when practicing technical analysis. These include volume, price, volatility, and support and resistance levels.

Volume determines whether there is enough interest in a stock to make it take off in a trend. It tells you how many other traders are interested in a particular stock and can confirm (or undermine) trends you think you see in the charts. In a nutshell, volume is the indicator that most accurately conveys the strength and depth of a trend. The success of a trader ultimately depends on his or her ability to decipher volume levels associated with price movements.

Volume is closely linked with liquidity, another important trading factor. If there is too little volume (an indication that no one is interested in the stock), liquidity is very limited. If volume is soaring, on the other hand, volatility is greatly increased, and you risk getting swept up (and perhaps away) in a rapidly moving market. Ideally, you are looking for a balance between these two extremes—enough volume to guarantee a liquid stock but not so much volume that you are chasing a moving price target.

There is no absolute volume that you should be looking for. You are only searching for an increase relative to what the stock has been doing. Rising volume indicates that interest in a stock is picking up. This rising interest means that the price is likely to move up along with the interest. If you see the volume of a particular stock falling, *sell!* This indicates that interest in the stock is waning, and whatever price trend was in effect is probably also changing. Remember, you want to be ahead of the trade, not behind it. Therefore, do not wait until all the other market participants begin to sell because at that point you may no longer be able to exit the trade. Millions of other shares will be headed for the exit gate, which is only wide enough for a few thousand. Rather, you want to sell while others are still buying, providing the liquidity you need.

The reason that volume is such an important indicator is that it is so closely correlated to price. Here are some signals to be aware of:

- A price rise accompanied by expanding volume is normal market behavior in a stock or index that is in an uptrend.
- Higher prices and decreasing volume signal a downtrend.
- A rally that occurs on contracting volume also can signal a downtrend.
- A final price/volume peak following slowly expanding price and volume can indicate that a trend is over.
- A lengthy decline in volume and price followed by a rally and another decline to the previous low volume and price signals the beginning of an uptrend. (In other words, it is a bullish indicator.)
- A stock that experiences a double-bottom model (a W formation) with expanding volume at and after the second bottom is also beginning an uptrend (a bullish sign).
- Decreasing price on increasing volume indicates a reversal of the previous uptrend.

The trading screen is your friend because it shows both real-time volume and real-time price ticks, bringing these two key indicators together and allowing you to follow their signals closely.

Volatility is a measure of a stock's average daily price range. If a stock's price changes very rapidly, it is very volatile. If a stock is not very volatile, it is not profitably tradable. On the other hand, if it is too volatile, it is also not profitably tradable. Once again, you must find a balance between two extremes.

There are two methods you can use to identify possible stocks to trade that have just the right amount of volatility. First, you can review various stocks' 50-day charts to determine which ones have average daily trading ranges of approximately $1. Another method is to select stocks each morning that are up or down at least 10 percent from the previous day. This 10 percent change often heralds an upcoming reversal in a stock's price.

Support and resistance levels are also very useful technical indicators. In fact, they are two of the most well-received indicators in charting stocks. Most professional traders look at these as viable analytical tools. So should you.

Support levels are floor trend lines (demand overwhelms supply), and resistance levels are ceiling trend lines (supply greatly overwhelms demand). The zone between these trend lines is known as the *trend channel*. When a stock bounces off the support line, rises to the resistance line, and then falls again, it is *channeling*. A very narrow trend channel indicates weak support and resistance. A wide trend channel indicates strong support and resistance.

Thus, how can you use these indicators to your advantage? There are two ways. First, you use them to determine when a stock is approaching a support or resistance level and thus a possible turnaround in price. Second, you use them to predict when a stock might make a breakout or breakdown, either by rallying past the resistance level or falling below the support level. In very simple terms, you want to buy stocks at the support level and sell at resistance. Remember, as a trader, you are looking to buy weakness and sell strength. Do not try to wait until stocks reach the very bottom of support or the very top of resistance, though. Chances are that you are probably not this good (few are), and you could incur serious losses by getting greedy. Do not get into a game of chicken. Try to buy stocks on their way down and sell them on their way up. And as mentioned earlier in the discussion of volume, market liquidity is also a key factor that good traders must consider constantly. If you wait until the stock price is almost at the resistance line, all the other market participants also will be trying to sell. You could end up unable to sell your shares, watching the stock price fall back down to the support level. Instead, you want to be selling when the rest of the market is still buying.

Before you put too much stock (no pun intended) in these levels, though, you should determine how strong they are. You must look at the amount of time that the levels have held as well as the number of times that they have been tested. Keep in mind that in the very short-term world of the day traders, sufficient support for a stock could come over a 10- to 15-minute period. Most intraday traders plot support and resistance levels using 1-hour intervals.

Using support and resistance levels wisely can give you amazing results. It is a technique that requires monitoring a level II screen so that you can observe the market makers buying when the stock nears a support level and selling when it comes close to the resistance level. If you notice that the market makers are reacting differently than usual, this could be an indication of an impending breakdown or breakout. If you do not recognize it, you can incur losses very quickly.

Beware: Support and resistance levels are natural barriers that are broken often. Stocks do have a tendency to resist breaking through the ceiling and falling through the floor, but these barriers are still very flexible. Once they are penetrated, stocks often will either soar through the roof (breakouts) or plummet very quickly (breakdowns).

Sometimes, when the resistance level has been broken, you may assume automatically that a huge breakout is about to occur. Wait a few minutes, though, because there could be a pullback. The stock could reverse its climb and begin falling toward support. You should only buy if and when the pullback moves above the resistance line a second time with strong volume. At this point, it is safe to assume that this stock is probably going to take off. In this case, many seasoned traders recommend getting a market order. You also can set a buy stop limit (through an ECN) at the price near the first pullback after the breakout.

Breakdowns follow the same pattern. A true breakdown is marked if the first pullback does not reach the support line. In such a situation, it is important to get short by selling into the buying market that creates the first pullback.

Becoming familiar with technical indicators and using them to glean information about specific stocks are key to your success as a trader. However, you also must be aware of broad market indicators. These are various signposts that you can use to predict the overall tenor of the market.

First, you must keep track of interest rates. You also must keep tabs on the Federal Reserve System and its actions. The Fed (overseen by the seven-member Federal Reserve Board) has many functions, but the one you should be most concerned with as a day trader is its role as an implementer of U.S. monetary policy. The Fed controls the growth of the U.S. economy, with a focus on controlled expansion. Why is this so important? Read the following two examples of unbalanced economic situations.

If a period of uncontrolled economic expansion occurs, increased availability of credit from the Fed to banks results in more liberal extension of credit from the banks to the private sector. Consequently, the private sector begins to grow very quickly. Higher earnings levels create a greater demand for labor. This increased demand for labor from a limited supply forces the private sector to raise the price of wages. As a result, goods and services become more expensive. This expansionary economic process is inflationary.

During a recessionary period, on the other hand, money is hard to come by. Growth decreases because the private sector is having difficulty procuring credit. As a result, firms suspend expansion projects until the cost of borrowing money decreases. Demand for labor is thus reduced, and as a consequence, the supply of labor increases. This larger labor pool puts a cap on wage pressures. The cost of goods and services remains unchanged. In an extreme recession, the cost of goods and services actually may go down.

As you can see now, the securities markets suffer when the economy is left to expand and contract on its own accord. The Fed is able to monitor the economy by adjusting the availability of funds in the U.S. banking system. This allows for sustained economic expansion and avoids the scenarios just discussed. The securities markets thrive when the general public believes that economic expansion is steady.

Oversold and overbought stocks are also useful signposts. If a stock has fallen past its former support level (a breakdown), you should see an opportunity in this overselling bandwagon. When the stock appears to be bottoming out past a former support level (when you notice a decreasing volume of sellers), this can be a good time to buy. Similarly, when a stock rises past a former resistance level (a breakout), you should see an opportunity in this overbuying bandwagon. You should wait until the buying volume starts to decrease and then seize the opportunity to sell the stock short.

The short-term overbought-oversold oscillator is a constantly changing average of net differences between advances and declines. It can be a very helpful tool in predicting near-term price movements of the market as a whole, as well as getting a feel for the current tone and future direction of the market. The short-term overbought-oversold oscillator should be reviewed on a weekly basis.

Upside/downside volume is a ratio of the daily up volume to the daily down volume. This ratio generally takes into account a 50-day period and is calculated by dividing the total volume on days when a stock closed up from the prior day by the total volume on days when the stock closed down. During bull trends, this ratio is up, and during bear trends, it is down.

The new-high/new-low index is a great broad market indicator because it mirrors the direction of the market in general. If it diverges from the general market trend, it alerts you that the move is suspicious. In jumpy markets, various composite averages may move in one direction, but the new-high/new-low index will fail to mirror it. In more stable markets, on the other hand, this index reflects the broad market trend.

As you can see, there are a number of analysis methods you can use as a trader. Especially if you are a day trader, you are going to use a lot more technical analysis to help your trading decisions. Do not be overwhelmed by the types of analyses available; just get to know a couple that comfortably fit into your trading style.

MARKET FUNDAMENTALS

There are certain things that every direct access trader should know about the markets. Direct access trading can be for anyone, regardless of past experience or lack thereof with the financial markets. However, you need to get familiar with the basic fundamentals of the market in order to be able to digest the wealth of information that is now going to be available to you. Then there are other rules such as discipline that have nothing to do with the market but are equally important in determining your success. Understanding market fundamentals is necessary so that you can put the pieces of the puzzle together when you make your trading decisions. By learning such things as who the players are in the market, the ways in which the general public reacts to certain types of news, and the key indicators to watch for, you will be able to make better informed trading decisions. Let's take a look at some of the basic market fundamentals.

The Markets

The two main markets for direct access traders are the New York Stock Exchange (NYSE) and the National Association of Securities Dealers Automated Quotation system (Nasdaq). Although most of the volume for direct access traders currently takes place on the Nasdaq, this will shift a bit over time as the NYSE becomes more "computer friendly" and less reliant on the old-world ways of trading stocks. The Nasdaq has become the direct access trader's exchange of choice because of the way in which the exchange is based on interlinked computers. This creates a much easier and quicker way for traders to enter and exit their positions. In addition, the Nasdaq has become the exchange of choice for most new Internet stocks, many of which have had tremendous gains over the last couple of years. Although the Nasdaq has only been around since 1971, it has grown in popularity very quickly and will continue to be the market of choice for direct access traders in the foreseeable future.

ECNs

Electronic communication networks (ECNs) have quickly become one of the most powerful tools in the financial world. Although they have only existed for the last couple of years, they have already had a significant impact on the U.S. trading markets, especially stocks traded on the Nasdaq. ECNs allow individuals to trade directly with other individuals and eliminate the "middleman." ECNs are in many ways like miniexchanges in that individuals congregate to buy and sell stocks. ECNs also have grown very quickly in popularity because individuals can use them to make trades after normal market hours. Even some of the large brokerage firms are starting to offer limited services for after-hours trading based on ECN technologies. Although new ECNs are emerging very quickly, in order for an ECN to be successful, it must have deal flow. Just as the Nasdaq and the NYSE need individuals to fill opposite sides of buy and sell orders, so do ECNs. If an individual is trying to sell 100 shares of YHOO on an ECN but no other individual in the marketplace wants to take the other side of the trade, then the market becomes illiquid. As a direct access trader, you can make trades on any ECN you choose. Usually your trading software will help direct you in terms of accessing the ECNs.

ECNs are one of the biggest reasons individuals can now be direct access traders. ECNs act as a private communications network that allows anyone to list his or her prices on the Nasdaq. What this allows individuals to do is bypass market makers and trade directly with other individuals. Market makers are the brokerage firms that place trades for their customers and trade for their own accounts. They often represent some of the biggest buying forces within a stock because of the large amount of capital they control and the large number of trades they make. A single market maker trade often can move a stock by a teenie ($\frac{1}{16}$) or an eighth ($\frac{1}{8}$). In fact, many day traders spend a significant amount of time trying to study specific market maker movements within a particular stock in order to profit on their moves. The number of ECNs has risen dramatically over the last 2 years, but each ECN acts like its own order book. The main ones include

All-Tech Investment Group	ATTN
Bloomberg Trade Book	BTRD
Brass Utility, LLC	BRUT
Instinet	INCA
Island	ISLD
Next Trade	NXTD
Spear, Leeds and Kellogg	REDI
Terranova Trading, LLC	TNTO

An ECN needs buyers and sellers to be able to provide liquidity or else it is of no use. ECNs traditionally were available mostly to institutions, but thanks to new software and the proliferation of the Internet, individuals are getting to take advantage of them as well. ECNs allow individuals to do numerous things that they could never do before. These include trading after market hours and avoiding spreads by trading directly with other individuals, along with being able to remain anonymous and essentially having a front row seat on Wall Street. ECNs are quickly becoming one of the biggest new forces in the world's financial markets. Although most people have not heard of them yet, it is only a matter of time before they will. A list of the major ECNs is given below:

INSTINET INCA

URL: *www.instinet.com*
SNAIL MAIL: 875 Third Avenue
                  New York, NY 10022
PHONE: 212-310-9500

Founded in 1969, Instinet has been in the business for some time. From its humble beginnings as an institution-to-institution trading firm, it has grown to include brokers. It is the world's largest agency brokerage firm, trading in over 40 global markets and acting as a member of 19 exchanges in North America, Europe, and Asia. It has more liquidity than any other ECN, and more traders view this ECN than any other private market. Instinet is registered with the U.S. Securities and Exchange Commission (SEC) as a broker-dealer and is a member of the NASD; all U.S. regional exchanges; the American Stock Exchange (Amex); the London, Paris, Toronto, Zurich, Hong Kong, Frankfurt, Stockholm, and Bermuda stock exchanges; the CBOE; and the European Options Exchange. Instinet's institutional equity clients own 90 percent of the managed institutional equity funds in the United States. In 1987, Instinet was purchased by Reuters.

As an agency broker, Instinet is neutral in its transactions, which means that it does not buy or sell securities for its own account. In addition, Instinet is able to lower transaction costs, specifically costs associated with market impact, which occur when a certain player becomes active in a stock. Instinet is able to lower market impact by providing anonymity for its clients, allowing customers to enter the market without divulging their identity. If you are widely known in the market, this can be a huge help because it prevents others from raising their prices when you enter your order. Instinet also helps to provide a more direct trading experience, allowing traders to interact directly with each other, to trade 24 hours a day, to route orders directly to exchanges, and to see how much a trade costs them in real time. When asked if they are actually a hidden exchange, Instinet smugly replies: "No more so than any large global broker."

ISLAND (ISLD)

URL: *www.isld.com*

SNAIL MAIL: 50 Broad Street, 6th Floor
New York, NY 10004

PHONE: 212-231-5000

EMAIL: *info@isld.com*

Island was founded in 1996 with the goal of creating an e-location for brokers and institutions to execute transactions. Since its inception, it has been widely regarded as one of the pioneers in real-time display, showing a real-time display of all its orders through the "Island BookViewer" technology. Island began representing orders in the Nasdaq's quote montage in January 1997. Its activity on the Nasdaq has been very large; usually, Island trades close to 200 million shares, or 12 percent of all Nasdaq transactions. Currently, it is the Nasdaq's largest market participant in Yahoo!, Intel, Qualcomm, Sun Microsystems, 3Com, and Oracle. These and other stocks enabled Island to have a trading volume of over 26.5 billion shares, with a dollar value of over $1.5 trillion in 1999. Island currently has over 350 broker-dealer subscribers. For a complete list of the firms that subscribe to Island, check http://www.isld.com/contact/matrix/index.asp.

Island currently is open whenever the primary equity markets are open for trading and accepts orders between 7:00 A.M. and 8:00 P.M. EST, but as demand increases, Island reports that these hours may be extended. Island currently accepts orders in increments as small as $\frac{1}{256}$ and has the technology to trade in decimals once it becomes the industry standard. While Island will accept increments of this size, it is best to check with your brokerage firm to make sure that it will allow this as well.

NEXTRADE ECN

URL: *www.invest2000.com*

SNAIL MAIL: 301 S. Missouri Avenue
                  Clearwater, FL 33756

PHONE: 727-446-6660

EMAIL: *pimge@sprintmail.com*

In November 1998, NexTrade became one of the first ECNs to receive SEC approval. With technology that allows customers to trade simultaneously with all ECNs and market makers, NexTrade serves a variety of financial institutions, including online brokers, market makers, mutual funds, hedge funds, and traditional brokerage firms. NexTrade is also well known for recognizing that traders are a different type of breed; in April 1999, NexTrade started staying open for business 24 hours a day, 7 days a week. Retail investors, through their brokerage firms, can now place limit orders for Nasdaq securities whenever they please. NexTrade also offers a matching session for NYSE-listed stocks from 5:15 P.M. to 9:00 A.M.

NexTrade is also known for having a high rebate in the market, at a quarter of a penny for each share of liquidity executed.

NexTrade also has pioneered the development of foreign currency trading platforms, recently developing Matchbook FX, in which it is a one-third owner (see Figures 5-1 through 5-5).

ARCHIPELAGO

URL: *www.tradearca.com*
SNAIL MAIL: 100 South Wacker Drive
Suite 2012
Chicago, IL 60606
PHONE: 312-960-1696

When the SEC altered its rules to allow ECNs, Archipelago was one of the first waiting in line. Archipelago was formed in December 1996 in response to the SEC's new regulations and was launched in January 1997 as one of the first original ECNs approved by the SEC. After creating new technologies, Archipelago jumped to a trading volume of 10 million shares per day, attracting Goldman Sachs and E*Trade, who soon became major investors. Archipelago has since gained such investors as Merrill Lynch and NBC. Archipelago appears on Nasdaq screens under the ARCA symbol and also offers access to the listed market.

Archipelago has put a great deal of emphasis on creating technology that people like. Traders are given anonymous access to the markets; orders entered into the system will be displayed as part of the ARCA bid or offer, whereas orders sent to other market participants will remain unidentified. Archipelago also has designed a national order book. Orders that are not marketable when they are submitted are placed in this book. Orders in the ARCA book can be matched within Archipelago or will be sent to other market participants. Archipelago also hypes its SmartBook software, which allows traders to find the prices they want by automatically delivering their order to the market participant who best matches. In addition, all this technology operates at high speed; pools of liquidity are connected in no more than 1 second.

Archipelago accepts trades during the hours of 8:00 A.M. to 8:00 P.M. EST. Visit http://www.tradearca.com/company/broker_access.asp for a list of brokers associated with the company. Currently, Archipelago is ven-

Figure 5-1 NexTrade home page. (*Courtesy of NexTrade.*)

turing to even further areas of online trading; in March 2000, Archipelago and the Pacific Exchange announced a plan to create the first fully electronic stock exchange for the NYSE, Amex, and Nasdaq stocks.

Bull Markets versus Bear Markets

Everyone knows it is always easier to make money in a bull market. If most stocks are going up, then your chances of making money are much greater, assuming that you are not shorting any stocks. However, the real

Figure 5-2 NexTrade 24-hour trading. (*Courtesy of NexTrade.*)

test for all traders is making money during a bear market because it becomes much harder to find good stocks to buy. Every direct access trader's strategy should change during such times. Overall market sentiment plays a huge role in the way stock prices fluctuate, and understanding when a shift is occurring in the market can be extremely valuable. This does not mean that you should pull all your money out of stocks when you see a couple of bad days in a row, but keep in mind the mentality of others seeing the same thing and how they might react. Fortunately for you, you will have the advantage of using direct access trading tools and being able to act instantly when the timing is right.

Interestingly enough, however, days when the market is down considerably often present one of the best buying opportunities for direct access traders. This is so because, come the next morning, if the market

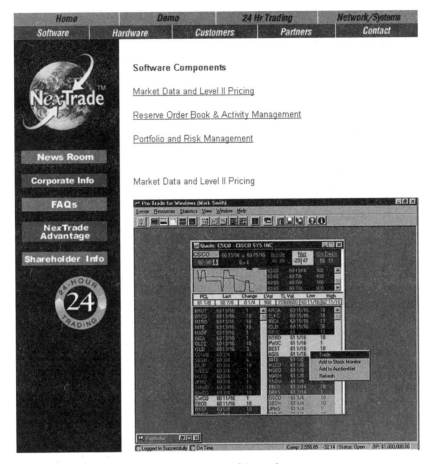

Figure 5-3 NexTrade software components. (*Courtesy of NexTrade.*)

shows signs of picking back up, there often can be great stocks to buy that may be priced below where they should be. For example, let's say that CMGI was down from 104 to 75 one day, and there was general news about the Internet but nothing in particular related to what CMGI is doing. The thing to do would be to pull up CMGI's chart and look where the stock has traded over the last couple of months. Has it been consistently on a bull trend, breaking new highs, or is the recent price of 104 per share a new high that maybe does not have much staying power? How has the stock reacted to similar news in the past? Has it rebounded the next day or leveled off at a new plateau? The key once again goes

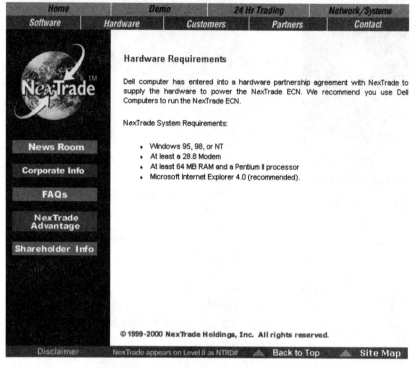

Figure 5-4 NexTrade hardware components. (*Courtesy of NexTrade.*)

back to doing your homework. Although the markets may only be open from 9:30 A.M. to 4:30 P.M., there is plenty to do to get ready for the next day or review your trades from the previous day. In order to capitalize on opportunities such as these, you really have to do your homework and be ready to find some "steals" in the market the next day. As one trader put it, "When the market takes a dive on any given day, I mean a real dive where almost everything is down, I come in the next morning licking my chops at all the bargains there are in the market." Although it is not always wise to wait for a "bargain" in the marketplace, when the situation does arise, it often can be a very good buying opportunity.

Level I, II, and III Quotes

Most people are familiar with level I quotes. These are the single numbers that appear the next day in the newspaper or on a Web site showing the current (but usually delayed) price of a stock and often the number of shares traded. A real-time level I quote is the same thing, although there is just no delay in the price of the stock. A level II quote is what is of most importance for direct access traders. Whereas a level I quote is like a snapshot of the price of a stock, a level II quote shows you all the real-time different prices for the bids and asks of a stock. Therefore, you can see the buying or selling pressure mounting within a stock at various prices. You also can see who the movers and shakers are within the stock, such as a specific market maker. This is one of the best weapons direct access traders have. Especially if you are making intraday trades, not using this information and trying to use level I quotes is like running with a cast on. It is just simply impossible to keep up. Level II quotes are for everyone, though. Who does not want to get in at the best price possible? If you are placing an order for 100 shares of MSFT at 110 and you see selling pressure mounting in the stock using your level II quotes and you wait an extra 5 minutes to buy the stock while it goes down to 105, you have essentially just saved $500 and can buy almost an extra 5 shares. Needless to say, level II quotes are a must for direct access traders. Level III quotes are for NASD firms that serve as market makers. They contain all the same information as level II quotes, but they allows market makers to also execute orders, make quotations, and send general information. Level III quotes are not really applicable to direct access traders. Level II quotes are where you get your edge.

Stock Symbols

For direct access traders, everything is about speed—getting information faster than anyone else and then being able to capitalize on it. This also ties in with knowing the symbols of the stocks you trade so that you can quickly pull them up. Although this may seem rather basic, it is very important for every direct access trader. In fact, many day traders often do not even know the name of a company but rather just the symbol they use to pull up a chart or other information on the stock. Regardless of what type of direct access trader you are going to be, get to know the symbols of your stocks so that they are second nature.

Data

Data are what give direct access traders their edge. Having the best data feeds, getting them in the quickest fashion, and making them easy to find on your screen are all extremely important. Data can be gotten from thousands of different places, and each trader has different types of data they like to use to make trading decisions. Direct access traders rely predominantly on technical analysis for shorter-term trades and fundamental analysis for longer-term trades. Although both will be discussed in greater detail later in this book, it is important to know that every trader has his or her own unique way to get information. Some may use only one or two pieces of technical information, whereas others may like to read commentary on individual stocks by key analysts. Some like to have the information on their screen color coded in certain ways, whereas others do not mind having to get the information manually themselves.

Long versus Short

Most direct access traders will tell you that you should almost always be going long unless you are a very experienced trader. The reason is that when you short a stock, or artificially sell a stock that you do not own in hopes that the price goes down, you are leaving yourself exposed to infinitely greater risk. A stock can go up forever, and as it continues to rise, you may have more and more trouble trying to sell your position. On the other hand, when you go long on a stock, in hopes that the stock will go up, it can only go to zero. Although this sounds horrible by itself, you would much rather go long on a stock at $10 a share and watch it go to $0 than to short a stock at $10 and watch it go to $100. If you purchased 100 shares, the difference is losing $1000 versus $90,000. Although this example is an extreme, it illustrates the greater risk associated with shorting stocks. This does not mean, however, that you should not eventually learn about shorting stocks and combine it with other techniques to make money in the markets. Many traders have done extremely well shorting stocks, although others bought Amazon.com or Yahoo! and are still waiting for the price to go down.

Record Keeping

It is always a very good idea to keep as accurate records as possible of your trading activity. Record keeping helps you examine both successful and unsuccessful trades and helps you to identify particular stocks on which you have made money over time. In addition, having neat records also comes in extremely handy around tax time. This alone will save you some money, and your accountant will thank you. And do not be afraid about your tax bill. It is also a good idea to keep track of your expenses. Get an understanding for where you are spending your money on things in addition to trades. Such other items as utilities, phone bills, data service fees, licenses, insurance, and accounting fees can add up quickly. Especially if you are direct access trading for a living, it helps to have a "business plan" so that you know exactly where you are spending your money and whether or not you are hitting the goals you set for yourself.

The more money you make, the more taxes you pay—so keep making money. It is a good idea to keep a set of files that list your trading activity either by stock, date, or some other mechanism. In addition, it is a good idea to go back frequently to examine your trades. Although some people at first feel that this is a waste of time, they quickly learn the value of doing so. For example, one of the best things about going back to look at both winning and losing trades is finding patterns in a particular stock and understanding the way the stock reacted to a particular piece of news. This sort of knowledge can be extremely handy when you are trading the stock again.

QUESTIONS TO ASK YOURSELF

1   Am I using basic analysis for long-term direct access trading, part-time day trading, or full-time day trading?

2   Which forms of basic analysis am I most comfortable using?

3   What will I be using these forms of analysis for?

4   What are the most important forms of basic analysis that I will need to spend time learning?

5   How comfortable am I with level II quotes and market maker movements, the most important forms of analysis for direct access traders?

6

TRADING FOR A LIVING

No one ever said trading for a living (successfully) would be easy. It requires discipline, focus, and training. You need to know going in that it can be a risky profession. Depending on whether you are going to be a day trader, a part-time day trader, or a long-term direct access trader, you have a different set of fundamentals to master. Everyone can benefit from learning the fundamentals of direct access trading. However, you need to be realistic from the beginning about your expectations and the amount of time you are going to be able to commit to it. There is obviously a much higher probability of success in using direct access trading tools than by trying to place the same trades through a third party such as any type of broker. However, if you want to get into trading more seriously, as in day trading, you need to get a really firm understanding of the people with whom you will be competing on a daily basis.

By some estimates, as many as 75 percent of day traders do not make any money. Trading does not need to be a losing proposition, but you need the right training. You only have to trade from 9:00 A.M. to 4:30 P.M. five days a week, but during this time, you have to be there 110 percent. It takes time to enhance your skills so that you can trade for a living. Many individuals start out as long-term direct access traders, master the fundamentals, and then commit themselves to spending more time with it. This is an especially good idea because it is extremely important that you love direct access trading if you want to do it for a living. Because it is such a fast-paced environment and you need to be improving your skills continually, it takes a real love for the markets to trade for a living. Do not be discouraged, however, if your background is not in the financial markets. Some of the most successful direct access traders have had no experience with the financial markets or even in general investing before they started. The key for all direct access traders who want to trade for a living is to keep your expectations realistic and your trading strategy conservative and use unrelenting discipline in the markets.

START SLOW

Keep your expectations low in the beginning. It can take up to 3 to 6 months to become profitable, depending on how quickly you master the fundamentals and get comfortable with such things as the keyboard. The best traders do not start out making $20,000 a day. This may be an average for the elite few, but when they started out, they may have only been making $500 a day. Then they moved up to $1000 a day, then $1500, and then one day they made $3000. However, remember that when you trade for a living, the name of the game is longevity. You would not walk into your boss's office and bet your entire annual salary on whether one project was going to be successful, especially when you do not control all the forces surrounding it. It is the same thing with day trading. A conservative approach, with the appropriate number of aggressive trades when the opportunities are exactly right, will make you a much more successful and even-keel trader over the long term.

Especially in the beginning, it is much wiser to make extremely conservative trades and only place trades when you are comfortable with the market factors. Although advanced day traders may place 50 to 100 trades over the course of a day, do not feel that you have to be nearly as active. If you make 1, 2, or 3 trades a day in the beginning, this is fine. You should be trying to interpret what is happening in the markets, looking for market maker patterns in a particular stock and getting comfortable interpreting real-time news and indicators. You can lose your shirt by being too eager in the beginning and be out of business in under a month if you are not conservative enough. Some new traders come into a hot market, buy a thousand shares of a stock, and watch the share price climb 4 points. They sell and make $4000. Then they write a bunch of tickets over the course of the day just so they are actually trading, and they end up basically breaking even.

Another big problem that new day traders face is that they make one big trade, make a couple of thousand dollars, and get overconfident. They try to replicate the same situation in another stock and end up taking on too much risk, losing more than they made on their last trade. In addition, new day traders especially have to become even more conservative when the overall volatility in the market heats up. The second a bit of choppy—or even down—market hits, a lot of new day traders get crushed because they get caught holding positions they hope are going to go back up. The key is to stick to your trading strategy, even if you are 100 percent positive a stock is going to go back up and it means taking a loss. Another important lesson for new day traders is to recognize when to take a profit. Stocks do not go up forever, and it is important to understand when the tide is turning in a particular stock and it is time to cash in. "Quit while you are ahead" is often a motto to live by in the trading world. You need to limit your upside to protect your downside. This is a conservative strategy, but it is what is going to give you longevity as a trader.

RISK

In its most fundamental sense, trading is risk management—and risk reward. You want to risk as little as possible to make as much as possible. When you are trading for a living, your number one objective is to keep your risk as low as possible while still giving yourself the greatest opportunity to maximize your investment capital. Controlling risk entails the ability to objectively monitor a couple of key indicators in particular. First, you must be able to judge the volatility in the markets. When the markets are more volatile, this means that there is a much greater chance that stocks in general are going to move in much greater ranges. Thus there is the opportunity to make or lose significantly more money. Another indicator is if the tide in the markets is moving toward a bull or a bear market. This can signify a time of great opportunity (bull market) or a time when you need to be more conservative in your trading strategy (bear market). And on a day-to-day basis, there are a number of other indicators that affect the overall risk to you as a trader. Your trading strategy should take into account how you trade during these time periods and set specific courses of action for you to take.

Each trader controls risk in a number of ways. The most common way is on an individual trade basis. Most traders are comfortable with about a 3:1 ratio. This means that they are comfortable risking $100 to make $300 or $500 to make $1500. Although this ratio varies from trader to trader, depending on how much capital they have and their risk comfort level, it is important to identify a ratio that gives you enough downside protection but also enables you to make the most of your capital. Once you decide on the ratio, you can use that same guide in every one of your trades. The key with every aspect of your trading strategy is embedding it in your brain so that you do not have to think about it. This leaves less room for emotions to enter the picture and enables you to be extremely disciplined, thus lowering your overall risk.

Remember that discipline is your best friend in controlling risk. As long as you always stick to your trading strategy, you will be able to control your overall risk and give yourself exponentially greater chances at a long and successful trading career.

HOW TO LEARN

You are presented with an enormous amount of information when you first start out as a direct access trader, let alone when you are considering trading for a living. Regardless of whether you have had any experience with direct access trading, it is a continual learning process because the markets are changing every day. Although traders who have been doing it for a while have an advantage in some respects, continually changing markets mean that only those who are on top of the market at any point in time will have the advantage. Therefore, remember that the more you learn throughout your whole trading career, the better you will be.

When starting off, it is best to go one step at a time. Master one skill, and then move onto the next. For example, when you begin, it is a very good idea to only go long and only in a particular way—such as putting bids in as a stock is going down or buying on the offer as a stock is going up. Then later you can move on to shorting. Shorting a stock inherently entails more risk, because a stock can only go down to $0, but it can go up to infinity. Many traders lost their shirts trying to short stocks such as Amazon.com, Yahoo!, and AOL. However, the ones with the appropriate risk strategies and discipline only lost some money, not their whole portfolio.

There is no sure way to learn how to trade for a living. The best way is definitely to be around other successful traders or at least garner insights from them in newsletters, seminars, and other forums. When you are starting out, however, there are certain "rules" that are a good way to get started. One of them in particular is to first learn to write 10 tickets a day without losing money. Then master writing 10 tickets a day while making a profit. Next will be 20 tickets a day with a profit. Your next goal will be making $500 a day. Then move on to $1000. Set realistic goals, and continue to push yourself. One day you will achieve $5000 a day. But do not try to jump in too quickly or you will never get to that day.

And never doubt that trading is something that can be learned. There are some people who pick it up more quickly than others, but no one just naturally *knows* how to trade. In some respects, it is like a video game that requires the development of a certain amount of hand-eye coordination. All players are presented with the same boards and the same number of lives, but the highest score is most likely going to go to the one who has played the most.

You should start out on a training module and learn the basics if you have never had any experience with direct access trading before. This will enable you to learn how to buy, sell, do executions on electronic communication networks (ECNs), the distinctions between ECNs, and basically get a feel for direct access trading. The best thing you can do in the beginning is master the basics—bids, offers, spreads, last prints, volumes, symbols, terms, and keystrokes—before you ever do a single, live trade. And when you do your first live trade, it should not be for more than 100 shares. You probably will do a basic buy on an offer and then look to sell it on an ECN as it is going up. If it does not go up, you will probably sell it on the Small Order Exchange System (SOES) or sell it through the select management ECN. Slowly get used to how stocks move because different stocks do move in different ways. The goal at this point is not necessarily to make money. You just want to gain as much experience as possible. The more hours you log in sitting in front of a computer watching stocks, the better you are going to get. You just need to get involved, try different things, and most important, limit your downside.

One of the most important things for new day traders to learn about is the concept of spreads. A *spread* is the incremental difference (in price) between the bid and the offer for a particular stock. Each stock has its own spread, which may fluctuate during the course of a trading day. It is a good idea not to get involved in anything more than a ¼ point spread in the beginning. And even though sometimes it is difficult, stay away from the Microsofts, Dells, and Ciscos of the trading world because they trade in sixteenths. They can be easy targets for new traders, but often you get faked out with these stocks because they move with no real rhyme or reason.

It is also incredibly important to talk to other traders. They are far and away your best resource at any point in your trading career. Once you have learned from the experience of others, you can start building your own experience. Being around experienced traders and asking them questions all the time is invaluable. By listening to them, you are able to see the techniques they use to analyze stocks, find out about other hot stocks in the marketplace, and get an overall sense of market sentiment. The key becomes learning to separate the good from the bad advice— because traders always have an opinion they are sure of. In addition, other traders are your best way to find out about other interesting stocks in the marketplace. There is a saying in the business: "If one person can watch 100 stocks and another person can watch 100 stocks, then two people together can watch 200 stocks." By helping one another, you can make each other better. This kind of communication is why the trading environment is so important.

You also should have a love of the markets and a fascination with them. This is part of what will push you to learn more and constantly improve your techniques and strategies. The best traders are the ones who *love* what they do, who *love* the market. And it is easy to learn from them because they also love to talk about trading. So just seek these people out and let them rattle on. You probably will disagree completely with some of them. With others, you will think, "That really makes sense. I agree with that line of thinking." Once you find a successful trader whose thinking seems to jibe with yours, learn all you can from him or her. Each new trader, however, really needs to form his or her own trading identity. Completely copying someone else's trading strategy just because they are successful is not the way to make it long term. You need to form your own trading strategy, with your own downside protections and key market indicators, so that you can adapt to the market as it changes. Every successful day trader in the world has a different trading strategy. Although they all look primarily at the same information and use a majority of the key indicators, they all have their personal strategies based on the risk-reward profiles they use to trade. A successful trading strategy is one that works and with which you are comfortable. It takes time to learn, however. Do not be frustrated if you have to modify your trading strategy every week when you first start, until you get the right fit.

WHAT'S THE SECRET?

There are no secrets. You should talk to other traders, learn how they trade, but ultimately, you need your own strategy. At a recent trading conference, a woman stood up during a panel entitled, "Secrets of the Top 1 Percent," and declared, "This is supposed to be a seminar on the *secrets* of the top 1 percent. I want to hear some secrets!" This is the wrong approach if you want to be a successful trader. You cannot go into this thinking that if you only crack the "secret code," you will make millions. There is a learning process involving a lot of hard work, and the "secrets" that work for one trader may not be the same ones that will work for you. In addition, those who expect to be making millions are the ones most prone for failure. They end up taking on too much risk in order to achieve their goals instead of gradually growing their capital base over time so that they can afford to make bigger trades later on. The best way to learn so-called secrets is to ask successful traders the top five trading rules they live by. These are the things that are embedded in their brains that they use to trade successfully on a consistent basis. Collect all the rules, and identify the top couple that fit the best into your trading strategy. Remember, in order for you to be successful, eventually you are going to need to come up with your own secrets. You will be amazed over time that this is not as hard as you may think. Every successful trader—and there are a lot of them—has his or her own special rules to make money in the markets.

TRADING ENVIRONMENT

There are people out there who have the discipline to teach themselves and push themselves. Do not assume, however, that you are one of them.

Many traders learn through experience that they do much better when they are surrounded by other driven, successful traders when they are trading for a living. The fast-paced environment pushes you to do better. A lot of it is based on competition. When you see the person next to you doing better than you, you are going to work harder to succeed, and you will also try to learn from that person in different ways.

Jeff Berline of Tradescape.com explains, "I can make a very good living by myself anywhere on the planet doing this. But I'm never going to push myself as much as if I'm in an environment with other successful people. I might be happy making $500 or $1000 a day when I'm working in a vacuum. As opposed to saying, 'Hey, there are guys making $20,000 a day and I'm stopping at $500!' When you look around, that's what's going to push you."

Other traders are your best resource. Learning from other people's experience is everything. Eventually, you can and need to rely on your own experience. But you must build your base over time, and in the beginning, your skill sets are obviously at their lowest. When you are helping each other, you are making each other better. It is important to be in an environment where people are shouting about stocks, talking about them, and expressing their feelings about them. It is also extremely helpful to be exposed to others' points of view, strategies, and styles.

A company called MarketSound has even gone so far as creating a simulated environment for traders because they recognize the motivation that lies in an exciting environment. It uses the actual recorded sounds of a trading floor and reads a live data feed into your computer to comment on market activity in real time. The bigger the trade, the louder are the "Buy 'ems!" When the market goes wild, the pit noise builds; when the traders go to lunch, it quiets down to a murmur. This patent-pending CD-ROM software not only motivates traders working from home but also allows them to use two senses rather than one. They can be listening to one market while looking at another. Some of the major trading firms for direct access traders are

> *Tradescape.com (www.tradescape.com)*. Tradescape.com has quickly emerged as one of the leading online brokerage firms and has developed technology that will soon redefine the industry. Founded in 1997, Tradescape.com sought to eliminate the gaps in time and information that prevented private investors from competing with Wall Street professionals. The company has created new technology, called the Electronic Communications Portal (ECP) and the

Smart Order Routing Technology (SORT), to do exactly this. The company provides direct connections to Nasdaq, the New York Stock Exchange (NYSE), and many ECNs, and their technology is able to review all these markets to get individual traders the best price. At this moment, this is the only firm that can route orders to multiple exchanges and find the best price available. Most mainstream online brokers send their customers' request to a market maker or ECN. With direct access, the individual investor can decide where to conduct trades, which allows for faster trades and cheaper commissions. Tradescape.com's commission is uniquely low. It takes only $1.50 for every 100-share trade. Tradescape.com processes over 100,000 trades a day and over $27 billion in transactions per month, creating a monthly trading volume that rivals America's largest online brokerage firms. Tradescape.com also has recently joined up with the Online Trading Academy to offer joint training courses on Tradescape Pro technologies (see Figures 6-1 through 6-4).

Specifics

- Accounts are $79.95 per month; this charge is free if more than 50 trades are made per calendar month and a $25,000 account balance is maintained.
- Commission is $1.50 per trade.
- Traders must have at least two of the following three requirements: $35,000 annual income, $50,000 liquid net worth, $100,000 in net worth.
- Minimum initial account balance: $10,000.
- Minimum daily balance: $5000.
- Traders must have at least 1 year of online trading experience or must have completed a direct access training course.
- One of the following operating systems is required: Windows NT/2000/98/95.
- One of the following browsers is required: Microsoft Internet Explorer 4.01 or higher or Netscape 4.72.

All-Tech (www.attain.com). All-Tech prides itself on being one of the first direct access trading firms and even touts CEO Harvey Houtkin as "the father of electronic stock trading." The firm has been actively involved in protecting and enhancing the rights of individual traders. All-Tech Direct's ATTAIN trading system sends trades right to the markets that traders choose, improving the

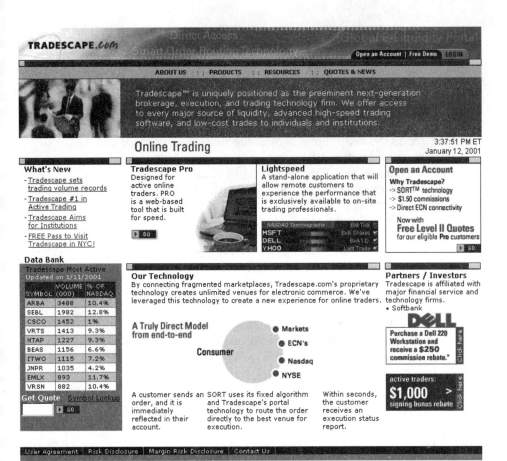

Figure 6-1 Tradescape.com home page. (*Courtesy of Tradescape.*)

chances of a better and faster execution. All-Tech offers two different types of direct access trading accounts: Attain Professional and
Attain Plus. Attain Pro offers a greater "horsepower" to the trader.
It has a very customizable trading platform, real-time level II
quotes and charts, and immediate confirmations. Attain Plus is a
more basic version of Attain Pro. Neither system has third-party in-
terference (see Figures 6-5 through 6-7).

Specifics

• For Attain Pro status, the cost is $250 per month (free with 100
transactions or more), with a $25 quote and order processing
fee. For Attain Plus status, the fee is $139.

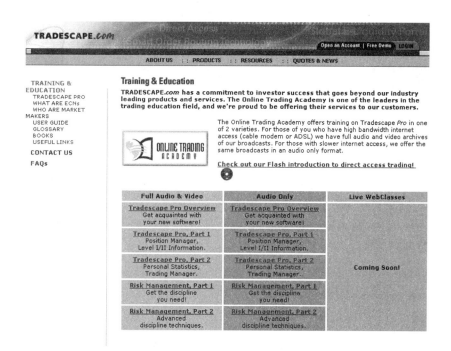

Figure 6-2 Tradescape.com training and education. (*Courtesy of Tradescape.*)

- For 1 to 2000 shares traded, commission is 0.5 cents per share; for trades greater than 2001 shares, commission is 1.5 cents per share. Other fees may apply for trades on the Nasdaq.

- Minimum balance of $25,000 for an Attain Pro account; minimum balance of $10,000 for an Attain Plus account. If traders are using Attain Plus for day trading, the minimum balance is $25,000.

- All-Tech recommends a Pentium II 200-MHz processor, 64 MB of physical RAM, and a 4-GB hard drive.

- Operating systems: NT Workstation 4.0 or Service Pack 5. Windows 95 and 98 may work, although less quickly.

CyBerCorp (www.cybercorp.com). CyBerCorp was founded in 1995 and was acquired recently by Charles Schwab. Since this change, CyBerCorp has grown tremendously. During the first quarter of 2000, trading volumes grew by over 80 percent compared with the

Direct Access
Smart Order Routing Technology

Global Liquidity Portal

Open an Account | Free Demo   LOGIN

ABOUT US   : :   PRODUCTS   : :   RESOURCES   : :   QUOTES & NEWS

Free Simulator

Tradescape Challenge is a powerful simulation of our online trading technology. It's easy to use, and there's no risk involved. Whether you've traded before or you're just getting started, this is your chance to experience all the features that Tradescape PRO* has to offer:

▲ SIGN UP FOR TRADESCAPE CHALLENGE

- Level II Quotes (delayed 15 minutes)- dynamic market maker and ECN movements

- Smart Order Routing Technology™ - scans the market for the best possible price

- Electronic Communication Portal™ technology - connectivity to the top market makers and ECNs in each stock.

- Dynamic market indicators - measures of strength and volatility

- Fast Executions

*The actual trading platform has some additional features, but this game will allow you to sample our product and get a feel for trading with Tradescape.com.

User Agreement | Risk Disclosure | Margin Risk Disclosure | Contact Us

Figure 6-3 Tradescape.com free simulator. (*Courtesy of Tradescape.*)

TRADESCAPE.com

ABOUT US :: PRODUCTS :: RESOURCES :: QUOTES & NEWS

ONLINE TRADING
FEATURES
PRICING
GETTING STARTED
USER GUIDE
FREE SIMULATOR
WHAT'S NEW

PROFESSIONAL
FEATURES

LEVEL II QUOTES
FEATURES
PRICING
GETTING STARTED

Professional Trading

Soon to be released online:

Lightspeed is the next generation of our FirstLevel™ trading software that is used by thousands of professional on-site traders. This stand-alone trading platform will allow remote customers to experience the superior software functionality and performance exclusively available to our on-site trading veterans.

To learn more about Lightspeed and when it will be available online please contact us at:
Lightspeed@tradescape.com

See Lightspeed in action

Learn more about Lightspeed's features

- **Direct Connections to ECNs and Nasdaq:** Gain a competitive edge with faster information and faster trades.

- **Smart Order Routing:** Seek the best venue for executing your trade.

- **Customization and Filter Consoles:** Choose the data you want, the way you want to see it.

- **Thermographs:** Track the direction and intensity of market movements.

- **ECP Book:** View the best bids and offers from every ECN, centralized in a single book.

- **Latency Console:** Know the speed of each ECN before you trade.

Figure 6-4 Tradescape.com market snapshot. (*Courtesy of Tradescape.*)

143

Figure 6-5 Attain.com home page. (*Courtesy of All-Tech Direct, Inc., ATTAIN Trading System.*)

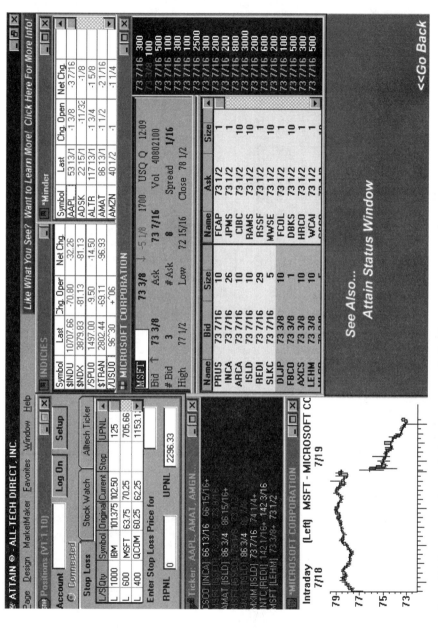

Figure 6-6 Attain.com products and services. (*Courtesy of All-Tech Direct, Inc., ATTAIN Trading System.*)

145

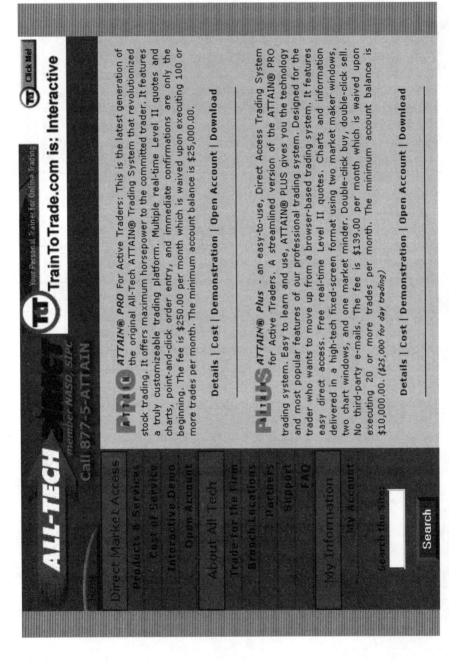

Figure 6-7 AttainDemoPC1. (*Courtesy of All-Tech Direct, Inc., ATTAIN Trading System.*)

previous quarter, making it one of the fastest growing online brokerage firms. In April 2000, over 30,000 trades per day were aver-
aged; a year ago there usually were 5000 trades per day. CyBer-
Corp offers three different platforms for traders. CyBerX is a basic
platform that is good for those new to direct access trading. Cy-
BerX2 has more advanced charting capabilities, streaming level II
data, and options trading. CyBerTrader includes CyBerX2 capabilities and adds multiple ECN books and more analytical tools. Using
this platform requires some previous direct access experience. Cy-
BerCorp also offers CyBerQuant!, a signaling tool that allows traders to search for stocks against over 90 different criteria.

Specifics

- Traders must have at least $10,000 in initial trading capital, an
  income of at least $35,000 per year, and a net worth of at least
  $65,000, exclusive of home. CyBerCorp also strongly recom-
  mends previous direct access experience or the completion of a
  training course.

- Commissions are flat fees ranging from $10 to $18, depending
  on the volume of shares traded. The fees are not attached to
  individual shares, however. There are no exchange fees charged
  for ECNs.

- CyBerCorp requires a 200-MHz processor, 64 MB of RAM,
  and 50 MB of free hard-drive space. Those using CyBerTrader
  must have a 266-MHz processor and 128 MB of RAM.

GRO Corp (www.grotrader.com). GRO Corp, founded in 1984 in
New York City to cater to active investors and professional traders,
now resides in Houston, Texas. It has since found its place in the
online trading world, focusing on individual investors. Traders trading Nasdaq stocks are able to choose where they would like their
trade routed; for listed transactions, GRO uses ABN/Amro to route
orders. These listed transactions will not be executed as quickly as
trades on the Nasdaq. The company does offer trading of securities
listed on the American Stock Exchange (AMEX) and the NYSE, as
well as options trading. GRO prides itself on customer service; it
has a full-time staff that is very responsive, and unlike many other
online brokerage companies, it lists its telephone number on its
Web site.

Specifics

- Traders must have a minimum account size of $25,000, or
  $50,000 in marginable securities.

- Monthly fees depend on the number of trades executed per

month. For nonprofessional accounts, traders must pay $200 if they make between 0 and 4 trades per month, $89 if they make between 5 and 39 trades per month, and nothing if they make over 40 trades. For professional accounts, fees are $327.50 if traders make between 0 and 4 trades per month, $216.50 if they make between 5 and 99 trades per month, and nothing if they make over 100 trades.

- Commission is a flat fee for trades under 5000 shares. For traders making 1 to 249 trades per month, commission is $17.95 per trade and 1.8 cents for every additional share over 5000. For traders making 250 to 499 trades per month, commission is $14.95 per trade and 1.5 cents for every additional trade over 5000. For traders making over 500 trades, the flat commission is $9.95 with a 1.0-cent commission on every additional share above 5000.

- GRO recommends a 450-MHz processor, 256 MB of RAM, an 8-GB hard drive, and either Windows 98, NT, or 2000.

ONLINE TRAINING

A number of new online training "schools" for direct access traders are starting to emerge. Remember, the number one way to get educated is to be mentored by a successful direct access trader (one willing to share his or her thoughts). However, online trading firms can be especially helpful if you cannot find such a person or make it into a direct access trading firm. The key when evaluating online training firms is obviously the quality of the instruction. What is the background of the teacher? Is the material prepackaged? Is there any one-to-one interaction either over email or the telephone? How do you ask questions?

Having some level of interactivity is extremely important. When you are just learning about direct access trading, you naturally have many questions, and you need to make sure that any online training site is going to be able to answer them for you. Remember, every one has a different strategy; therefore, answers will vary, and you should never take anyone's advice as cast in stone. However, if you can find an online training site that offers a class or package that suits your needs (and at a fair price), then it may be well worth it. Especially when you are starting, the best education is learning by hearing other traders talk. Whether this occurs in person or through online education, it helps you to begin to understand the mindsets of different types of direct access traders. Remember to take all advice with a grain of salt, however. Every single direct access trader has a different strategy. Take bits and pieces away from the ones you think have hit on something, but do not be afraid to completely disagree with others as well, even if they are highly successful. A person's trading strategy is largely determined by his or her comfort with various risk levels. Thus it is necessary to customize your own strategy from the ground up.

A TYPICAL DAY

When you are trading for a living, it is important to get into routines. This will improve your discipline and allow you to enhance your knowledge every day, instead of being in a million different places and never really learning about any one or group of stocks. Successful traders have become successful because they have developed a personal strategy that works for them on a daily basis and which they update over time.

Each day you should have a list of stocks that you intend to follow. This list generally will stay the same, but it also should evolve slowly over time. Some stocks will be omitted; others will be added. A good rule of thumb when you are just starting is to look at about 15 stocks the first thing every morning that you think you might trade. This list may change daily, based on other interesting stocks you learn about from other traders or the fact that a stock on your list has become too volatile or too docile. It is extremely important, however, not to have too long a list. If you try to cover too many stocks, it is impossible to develop an "understanding" of any given stock. Over time, your capacity to monitor more stocks will enhance, but start small in the beginning and learn the fundamentals about how to analyze these stocks. Some traders like to follow stocks all in one industry, whereas others favor sampling from a couple of different industries. The key is to understand the volatility of each of these stocks and how you need to act accordingly. It also is a good idea in the beginning to try to follow a group of stocks that all have similar trading characteristics, especially with respect to volatility. Over time, you can begin to trade more volatile stocks, but you should keep your risk level as low as possible in the beginning. Let's take a look at what a trading day can be like for a day trader:

Trader Speak: Jeff Berline (Tradescape.com)

8:45–9:15 A.M. Evaluate the "core 15." Look at what they did the day before, and try to predict what they will do today. For example, if the market got crushed yesterday and there's a stock that went up a little or stayed flat, you should look at getting involved in that stock first thing in the morning if it is an up day or an up run. Chances are that such a stock is going to be strong. Similarly, if there is a stock that was very weak yesterday, you should look at shorting it in the morning.

Before the market opens, you also should look for particular new stories that came out overnight and stocks that are releasing earnings. This helps you prepare mentally and get an understanding for what will be fueling the movement of specific stocks. You want to get a grip on every significant piece of information that could affect your core 15. Remember that even news that may be stock- or industry-specific could play a significant role in affecting your stocks. Things such as inflation numbers, employment reports, and other types of reports often have an impact on the markets as a whole.

9:15–9:30 A.M. See what is active. Go to a risers and fallers list and see what is hot in the morning. Check out what they are talking about on CNBC. See who is doing premarket trading in particular stocks, and get an understanding for why those stocks are being traded. Some traders establish a position before the open and have success with it. However, this is extremely unpredictable and really only occasionally a good move for very experienced traders. As a general rule, do not trade anything before the open unless you have a position that you came in with from the day before.

9:30 A.M.–4:30 P.M. You are continually monitoring the core 15, pulling up their level II quotes and intraday charts and looking for their support and resistance levels. The key is to try to find the range in which the stock is trading. When a stock is trading within a certain range, you try to make a little bit of money within that range when you start to get an understanding of the movement. When a stock breaks out of a range—up or down—you respond accordingly.

For example, let's say that a stock is very strong. It has been strong for days, and it is one of the stocks you have been following, so you know it pretty well. It has been trading between 74 and 76. You may look to buy or sell 100 shares within this range. Buy in the 74 range, and sell around 76. When you see a break above 76, this is when you buy as much as you can get. If it stops right there and does not continue to climb, you sell as much as you can. You are looking for the stock to go up to 77 or 78. This is when you will make your biggest plays. On the other hand, if it breaks down below 74, you start intensely watching it for a bottom. Every stock you have on your list should be on that list because you think it is a strong stock. You are looking for stocks that are trending up over at least a 30-day period. Thus, if this stock breaks down below 74, start testing it by throwing in bids. Lay off at the initial breakdown below 74. But when you start to see it slow down—there are more market makers on the bid, there is more size of stock at the bid—start to put in bids to see if people are hitting them.

5:00 P.M. When the markets close, immediately write down your profit or loss, how many tickets you wrote, and the average. Basic information will come on a hedge report, but you also should have your own personal record in case there is any discrepancy. Then go to an administrative module, which will show you a breakdown of where you made your profit (or loss). Write down any stock on which you made over $500. For the losers, just try to figure out why you lost. Usually, it will be pretty clear, and you will remember, but it is good to refresh your memory as to why you lost money on a particular stock. For the winners, pinpoint how you won. Then the next time maybe you will make a bit more. If there is a stock on which you made money that is not on your list, add it to your list. If there are stocks on your list that you have not traded in 3 or 4 days, cross them off the list.

CHOOSE STOCKS WITH DIRECTION

If you want to take a relatively conservative, safe approach to trading, you should avoid stocks that are all over the place. There are definitely possible gains in them, but if the risk-reward ratio is too high, it is not worth it. This does not mean that all "crazy stocks" should be avoided. A stock may be up 20 points and be very methodical in the way it climbed. The stocks to shy away from are the ones that are up 15 and down 15 with no rhyme or reason.

Large-cap stocks such as Microsoft, Dell, or Cisco also can be hard to trade. It takes massive amounts of buying and selling to move these stocks, so they are going to move in a smaller range, and again for often no apparent reason. What is going to make Microsoft go up a point versus down a point? This is really hard to know at times. However, stocks such as these can be some of the best ones to start to learn on because your exposure level is so much smaller. It is a good rule of thumb, however, that the higher the price of a stock, the more it can move. For example, new full-time day traders should start out not trading anything over $50 a share. This will lower their risk while still allowing them to get a feel for trading.

HOLDING LONG-TERM POSITIONS

If there is a stock that you want to hold onto long term, it is probably best to get it out of your trading account. The volatility of stocks these days makes it very difficult to look at the day-to-day text of one particular stock and not be tempted to sell. Even the best-performing stock has its down days. As discussed earlier in this book, it is absolutely necessary to keep your day trading money and other investment capital very separate. It can be all too tempting to "put everything you own" into a position that you are absolutely sure of. This is a disaster waiting to happen, however. Holding long-term positions is an excellent way to hedge your overall trading risk. By buying the right long-term positions, you can offset some of your trading risk with the stability and growth of other investments. The key, however, is to have enough discipline to keep the two pools of money separate and allocate appropriate amounts to each.

HOW DO YOU MEASURE YOUR SUCCESS?

Each trader has a different way to measure success. Some simply set monetary goals at the beginning of every month, whereas others simply look to see how closely they followed their trading strategy. Others simply wing it, although we would not advise this for anyone. Research shows that individuals who do measure success and identify ways to attain it have the best chance for success over the long term. Remember, the key part of this sentence is *over the long term*. It can be fairly easy for anyone to go out and have a great day, making large and risky trades, but in all likelihood they have had numerous very bad days trying to get their one great day. Trading like this will make you extinct in a short time. Trading is obviously a very monetarily oriented profession. It is important to step back from the day to day, though, and measure your success on a wider scale. When you are first starting to trade for a living, however, your goal should be to not lose money every day. Individuals who are able to "survive," meaning not run out of money in the first 3 months, have the greatest chance for success. Therefore, do not look to make a killing— or even anything—in your first couple of months. Instead, look not to lose money—and get a feel for the markets—so that you can start making larger trades once you have more experience behind you. Try setting a goal every week, month, or quarter. If you reach that goal, then move up to a higher goal. Measure your success by watching the numbers go up. You have to continue to push yourself, to push your goal. This is when you really feel the success and the security.

WHAT KIND OF BACKGROUND DO YOU NEED?

Successful traders come from all different walks of life. You do not have to be an Ivy League college grad with a degree in finance to make a living as a trader. There are definitely many traders who fall into this category, but there are also former surfers, homemakers, engineers, and others. The key is to get a feel for what trading is like. Are you intrigued by the markets? Can you afford to risk the investment capital? Do you really enjoy the trading environment? Can you handle the stress? These are the most important questions for new day traders, not where they were educated. If you feel comfortable will all the preceding questions, then you have a chance of success. There are no guarantees in this business, but for those who do succeed, there is no better job in the world.

No specific educational or professional background is required to be a full-time day trader. What you do need are specific personality traits. You need to have the spirit of an entrepreneur. In this line of work, you are your own business. This is why the environment is so important. You need to push yourself, and for many people it is difficult to stay motivated when you are working alone. Once again, you must have the inner discipline to be able to motivate yourself and set goals. Responsibility is also very important. You cannot say, "Well, I only really need to be working from 9:30 A.M. to 4 P.M." or "I don't have to work today." If you owned your own business, you would take it more seriously than this, and this is how you should treat trading for a living. It takes time to become successful, and you need to be willing to put in the effort.

You also should have a competitive spirit—either with others or just with yourself. You have to have this competitive edge to give you the drive to push yourself and excel. Trading is a very competitive profession. It is like a sport in a lot of ways, where you are competing head to head with other individuals all across the world, pitting your knowledge against theirs and seeing who will come out ahead. You cannot see these competitors, but they are out there, and whether you are up or down for the course of the day lets you know if you are winning or losing. However, it is important for all day traders not to think of the money they are making or losing over the course of a trading day. Think of the number on your screen as simply the number of points you have. It can be too damaging mentally if you start to think, "I just lost this month's rent" or "Now I can go on vacation to Bermuda." Successful day traders block out the money and only think about the trade at hand. Teach yourself to do this from the beginning.

Psychologically, you should be able to accept the fact that you are going to have losing trades. You have to be able to learn from losses and move on without getting down on yourself. A positive mindset is key. Once you start to become negative, you will lose more and more trades. You must start with a fresh head every trading day. When you have a bad day, go back and review what you did wrong. When you had a great day, go back and review what you did well. Trading is a very psychological profession. You are matching your wits with the rest of the world, trying to understand the way institutions, individual investors, and other traders are going to react to technical indicators and fundamental news.

Insecurity is a trader's worst nightmare. Most people associate losing money with fear. As a professional trader, you do not have this option. To a certain extent, you have to separate yourself from the money. It is just numbers, just odds. You can flip a coin 100 times and it could be heads 100 times, but eventually, the odds are going to even out. You have to keep telling yourself this. Just because you hit a streak of bad trades does not mean that you can get negative. You must keep a positive frame of mind. Tell yourself that you are going to take all that you have learned and make smart trades. Do not try to get it all back in one shot—this is when you can get hurt. A trader who gets scared and antsy is a trader who is going to fail. Confidence is a trader's best friend. Just make sure to use it with the right amount of discipline and a realistic trading strategy.

HOW MUCH DO YOU NEED TO GET STARTED?

How much money you need to get started is really a function of how much you can afford to lose. We recommend to every trader that you should only use money that you can afford to lose, mostly because you really cannot expect to make money during your first 3 months as a full-time day trader. Sometimes it can even be 6 months before you become profitable. But this does not mean that you have to lose money. And once you get over the hump, you can make up for the difference very quickly. Thus you do have to be in a financial position where you can afford to have no income for a 6-month period or even longer. As far as capital, it does not take very much.

In today's market, several stocks often jump up 20 points. Frequently, you will look at the risers and fallers list and see that the first 45 stocks are up more than 10 points. This amounts to a lot of stocks to trade that are moving very quickly. Although many of them are over $200, you can still find a lot under this price. With a $200 stock and a 2:1 margin, you only need $10,000 to trade it. Thus really, $10,000 can be enough if you are trading on a 2:1 margin. However, remember that in the beginning you really should not be trading such volatile stocks. You should be trading much smaller stocks that have a much smaller chance of moving in such large increments. Although you will not make as much, you also will not lose as much—and this is the golden rule when you start trading for a living. Lose as little money as possible in the beginning; do not concern yourself with trying to make a big splash. In addition, remember that in the beginning you should not be trading more than one stock at a time. You have to focus on enhancing your skills as a trader in the beginning so that when you are trading larger amounts later on, you have the fundamentals down pat. Do not be tempted to trade riskier stocks or a greater number of stocks in the beginning just because the person sitting next to you is making a killing. This will come in time if you learn the fundamentals and trade very conservatively in the beginning.

HOW DOES EXPERIENCE HELP YOU?

They say in the industry, "Past performance is not indicative of future results." This means that you can never get too comfortable. Just because you have made good trades and been successful monetarily for a few months does not mean that you can get lazy.

This idea can be misleading, however, because it does not acknowledge the reality that patterns in this industry do repeat themselves and that experience is extremely valuable. Once you have seen something happen once, you can make a calculated judgment the next time you see the same warning signs. As a professional day trader, you analyze what is happening in the moment and compare it against your own personal database of all the things you have seen. Based on this experience, you predict what will happen next and place your trades accordingly. The best indicator you have as a trader is how a stock reacted in the past to similar pieces of market news or the way a stock has reacted to previous price levels.

Sometimes a stock will not do what you expect. This is the true test of a good trader. You cannot let emotion get involved. If a stock is not doing what you were expecting, change your position—if you bought it, sell it; if you are short, buy it back. Limit your downside. Sometimes this will limit your upside, but overall, it is worth it. You must incorporate this into your trading strategy. New traders especially get into the most trouble waiting for a position to go their way. They are 100 percent sure that the stock will come back up, so they wait it out and lose more and more money. Good traders sell their position and buy back in at a new lower level with which they are comfortable. Good traders do the same thing on the upside as well. When they have a winning position, many sell enough of their shares to cover their initial investment and then wait out the rest until it decreases a certain predetermined amount, where they sell it all and move on.

There are times when you will sell a stock and shortly thereafter it will do exactly what you had expected originally. This can be momentarily frustrating, but it is better than losing $500 or even $5000. You want to have as few losing trades as possible. They will happen, and you need to be able to move on—but you must limit your losses. Your losers can even be more than your winners, in terms of quantity, but you must make more money on your positive trades than what you lose on your negative ones.

STAY FLEXIBLE

Day trading is a very dynamic profession. You need to evolve as the market evolves because even the most successful traders currently will disappear if they do not update their trading strategy as the market changes. Use the past as a guide, but be prepared to adapt your strategy for the future. You may reach a point where you are making $5000 a day without much effort. It is almost easy. You are very comfortable. Then, suddenly, the market changes, and you are losing money. You need to recognize the need to take a step back, to get some perspective, and reassess your strategy. Most traders analyze their trading strategy on a weekly or monthly basis in order to identify these trends. Often, you will need to start over in many respects, although your learning curve will be much less steep. Reset your goal to staying positive; maybe $5000 just is not realistic anymore. Then set your goal at $500 or $1000. After a little while, you will understand the new dynamics of the market, and you will be up to $5000 again. However, you must be willing to hit that "reset" button and realize that the same strategy is not going to work forever.

LONGEVITY

Trading can be the greatest job in the world. You work your own hours, answer to yourself, and have the opportunity to make as much money as possible. However, you have to remember that in order to succeed in the long term, you must have a firm dedication to understanding the markets every day. Persistence is key if you want to achieve longevity as a day trader. You have to trade *every day*. The longer you are away from the market, the harder it will be to catch up. Especially in today's dynamic environment, you really cannot afford to step away for too long. You miss too much.

Trading is a job just like any other job. You are going to have your ups and downs. Sometimes you are going to love your career, and sometimes you are going to hate it. But it *is* a career, so you need to give it the time and respect that it deserves if you are going to be a success and last for a significant amount of time.

And overall, you need to really *want* to be there doing this day in and day out. If this is not the case, then this is probably not the profession for you, and you are not going to last. It can be tedious sometimes. It can be frustrating a lot of the time. But when it comes down to it, you need to love it. There are people making decent livings as traders who are just doing it for the money, but all the supersuccessful traders who make it over the long haul are the ones who love it.

WHAT ARE UNSUCCESSFUL TRADERS DOING WRONG?

Some of the biggest losses in the trading industry stem from pure stubbornness and lack of discipline. Sometimes traders get too aggressive and start to average down a position. Then, when the unexpected happens, it becomes an enormous loss that they cannot cope with. At other times traders simply do not follow their trading strategy. They succumb to their emotions and start trading out of their zone. At still other times a trader is simply out of touch with the markets. Maybe he or she just needs to take a step back and start analyzing one or two stocks again to try to get an understanding for the way the market is moving these stocks.

Many unsuccessful traders are just too emotional about trading as well. You can compare the problem with that of a professional athlete who allows his or her mind to get in the way of his or her performance. An example would be a kicker who misses three in a row and on the fourth tells himself, "I can't make it. What am I doing?" If this is your attitude, you are completely sabotaging yourself. A positive frame of mind is essential in this business. When you see someone getting into a negative mindset, you watch them start going downhill. Although there are flamboyant traders in the world, most successful traders are fairly reserved, at least while trading, and they concentrate only on what is happening on their screens.

CHANGES IN TRADING

ECNs have not been in existence for very long. They have brought a lot of liquidity to the market, but they also have made it trickier. The option to make a trade using any of the different ECNs means that you have to know which ECN to use and when. There are many smaller ECNs that you want to avoid. They do not have a lot of volume, and you can get trapped holding onto a trade longer than you want to because there is no buyer or seller. There is always immediate execution on larger ECNs like Island. As discussed in Patel, *Direct Access Execution*, each execution method has its own unique advantages and disadvantages. The key remains knowing which ones to turn to first and how to use them all to your advantage.

In addition, stocks today are a lot more volatile, and professional traders are making more money than ever before. The top 50 stocks are moving 10 points or more. For the people involved in these stocks, they are huge moneymakers. However, this means that there is that much more risk and competition as well. And this means that updating your trading strategy and sheer discipline are more important than ever. Although there are more people trading in the markets than ever before, the stakes are also higher than they have ever been before.

The changes in trading can be difficult for people just getting into it now if they do not have the proper training. In some ways, coming into it today, you can have a jaded view of the market. You might figure,

"Hey, there's a stock up 20 points every day. Why don't I just buy 1000 shares of that stock?" This can be really dangerous if you do not consider the downside. The stock also could go down 20 points. Just because there is a bull market does not mean stocks cannot go down. New traders can get hurt very quickly these days if their eyes are too big for their plates. Thus it is particularly important in this market and this trading environment to *start slowly*. Learn to be positive. Learn to write 10 tickets a day without losing money. Then learn to write 10 tickets a day when making some money. Then try to make $500 every day—or at least average $500 a day at the end of the week. Then try to do $1000 a day consistently. Thus you continue to push yourself no matter how high you get, but you do it methodically. Do not get overeager. This is when you lose money. There is a lot more risk out there today, so you need to be extra cautious as a new trader.

THE CONSERVATIVE APPROACH

A conservative trader looks to limit his or her losses before he or she looks to reap huge gains. More aggressive traders say that you must run with your winners. And this is true to a certain extent. Obviously, you do not want to continually sell your good trades and good positions and hold onto your losers. Then you are going to get killed. The conservative approach will limit your upsides to a certain extent, but it also will keep your downsides in check. If you are a conservative trader and your goal is to be up $5000, you will stop when you get there. You would rather stay at 5 than risk going down to 3 by trying to make 7.

As a new trader, you have to start out conservatively. The "aggressive" traders you may see and hear about did not start out that way. They grew into it. They too started out making $1000 a day, progressed to $2000, and eventually made it up to $3000. Now they may be making $20,000 a day, but they have been doing it a *long* time. For them to suffer a $30,000 loss one day is comparable to a new trader suffering a $1000 loss. It is all relative. You have to find the level at which you are comfortable. You cannot necessarily look at the person next to you and think, "He just took a $10,000 loss and I only took a $1000 loss. I'd rather be me." Maybe his daily average is $20,000 and yours is only $2000. Focus on yourself, not on anyone else. The only comparison you should ever look at is how much you achieved relative to your goals.

WHAT TOOLS DO YOU NEED?

You must have a direct access system with level II quotes and access to all the ECNs. Level II screens let you see not only the inside quote but also the underlying bids and offers. It gives you a lot more information with which to make an educated trade. Without this you will never keep up with the best traders. You may be able to make money sitting at home on Ameritrade, but you will have the opportunity to make 10 times that on a level II system.

You also should have a news service and TV so that you can listen to CNBC all day. Your computer should be top of the line and have a high-speed line to the Internet. Execution speed and quote speed are also key. Even a split-second wait to receive a quote can lead to a huge loss— hundreds or even thousands of dollars. This means having the appropriate connection such as a T-1 line or a digital subscriber line (DSL). Do not even bother with a conventional modem. It is too slow, and the split-second advantage is going to make all the difference.

You can set up these tools in your home or go to an actual day trading firm. Although many individuals do trade from home, we recommend for individuals trading for a living to seek out an environment where there are other professional traders. This environment can be extremely helpful for a number of reasons. As we mentioned before, it is impossible for one individual to keep an eye on everything that is happening in the markets. Other traders will help you spot new stocks to trade and be great sounding boards for your analysis. In addition, and most important, learning from other traders is the best form of education. Look for a successful trader to take you under his or her wing and teach you some of the fundamentals, or at least ask to sit near him or her so that you can soak in as much as possible. However, remember that although this is the best way to learn, you must start to come up with your own trading style. Many new traders fall into the trap of trying to mimic their mentor closely and then not being able to perform when they are out on their own or the fundamentals in the market start to change. Learn everything you can from your mentor, but use this information to build the foundation for your own trading strategy.

Even if you are not doing solely intraday trades, you should be using direct access trading tools. If you are doing more than 10 trades a day (even if they only amount to 1000 shares total), it is crucial to have direct access to the markets so that you can get the best information and price for every trade. Without a direct access system—looking at level II quotes with access to all the ECNs—you are not a professional trader. You must trade in real time in the live market. With snapshot quotes (as with traditional online investing firms), you are not seeing the current market price. And considering the speed with which market prices can change these days, even a few seconds can make a huge difference.

DISCIPLINE

Discipline is everything. You must commit to the fundamental rules that you set for yourself. No rules are set in stone, so you have to formulate your own and stick to them. One of your rules might be to never take big losses. Or it might be to consistently look at stocks that you are writing a lot of tickets in but not making any money on and commit to stop trading those stocks. This can be hard to do sometimes because these stocks have become sort of your "pet stocks," but if you have made such a rule, you have to stick to it. You have to maintain the discipline to go over your numbers and change the way you trade accordingly.

You can still try different things. You can learn a lot from the person training you about how he or she makes money. For the most part, however, you must find what works for you and stick with it. You also have to be willing to change and bend and grow because the market is a dynamic place. Different things work for different people. There are some people who are solely short traders. There are others who only trade long. There are some people who do both. Some people make their money because they are right one in five times, but when they are right, they have 5000 shares that go for a run. They do very high ticket volume because they buy a lot of each stock, and when they are wrong, they get out quickly for as little loss as possible. When they are right, they let their winners go, and they make $10,000. Their strategy is based on the idea that sometimes they will make $10,000 or $15,000 a day, and sometimes they will lose $5000 or $8000. But they will be right a lot more than they are wrong. Other traders do not take losses very well, so they do not write as many tickets. They are not willing to take the $2000 loss to see if it becomes a $5000 gain.

Experience will bring you confidence as a trader. This is all that it takes—doing it day after day. Somewhere along the line—after 3, 6, or 9 months, or even a year—a light bulb goes on in your head, and suddenly you realize that you know what you are doing. You feel confident.

When you start making money consistently over time, you become confident, and confidence is a key to trading. Once true confidence is instilled, you can take a loss, even a big loss, and still rest assured that deep down you know how to make money. You have made a mistake, done something that could have been avoided, but you still know how to trade. Remember, even the most successful traders are only right 50 to 60 percent of the time on average.

The importance of building confidence is why it is so important to move slowly. First, set a goal of being positive. Then $500 a day. Then $1000. Then do $1000 every day for a month, and it will become easier and easier. You cannot just average $1000 one day and then the next day aim for $2000. You have to take it slowly. Realize that it could take more than 6 months to get up to an average of $2000 a day. And once you are confident, you can push it up a level. This may mean trading more or getting involved in different stocks or buying more shares of the same stocks. Whatever it is, it is doing the same thing you have come to know, but pushing it up a level. If you push too much and it does not work, you still have the confidence to go back and do what you were doing before.

One of the things many traders value most about their jobs (as much as the possibility of it being very lucrative) is being their own boss. You can make a lot of money without having to answer to anyone. Whether you make money or lose money, it is all up to you. No one else can be held accountable. This can be a very good thing for a lot of people, but it requires discipline in order to succeed. Just because you are your own boss does not mean that you can skip work just because you do not feel like working. Successful traders treat their jobs just as if they were a doctor and had no choice but to go to work every day, focus, and do the best they can. Even though the hours are good by a lot of measures, the intensity and focus required during the hours when the markets are open are unlike any other job. In addition, it can be very difficult to want to stay after having a good or bad day and review your trades. You must get yourself into habits that will allow you to keep learning and become a successful trader.

If you are not willing to be there day in and day out, this is probably not the profession for you. Just because you are your own boss does not mean that you can take off every Friday. You have to love it and be dedicated to it to be successful. There are people making decent livings trading who are only in it for the money. But the extremely successful traders *love* what they do. They love the market, and they love trading. They love the excitement, the action, the first-row seats to the adrenaline of Wall Street. Remember, today you have the same access to the same markets as Solomon Brothers, Goldman Sachs, or Smith Barney.

WHAT HAPPENS IF THE MARKET CRASHES?

If the market crashes, it is not good for anyone, but direct access traders will have the best ability to exit their positions. In fact, many day traders yearn for days when the market is down substantially because they come in the next day able to buy stocks at "cheap" prices. Because most other individuals are still left holding their positions or have taken huge losses, day traders are in a very enviable position.

In the long run, a market crash is obviously bad for everyone. In the short term, however, direct access traders actually could make a lot of money off a crash. There is usually a lot of activity following a crash, and traders thrive on this and can take advantage of it. A market crash will not end day trading as we know it. Day trading will change over the years as more and more individuals get direct access to the markets, but there will still be enormous financial opportunity for professional traders for a long time to come.

RULES TO LIVE BY

Every professional day trader has his or her own rules to live by. It is often a good idea when just starting out to ask a couple of other successful traders what their rules are. Depending on your experience level and capital base, your own set of rules obviously will vary accordingly. Below are some of the rules used by two of the leading traders at Trade-scape.com:

- Do not get too emotional.
- Remain disciplined at all times.
- Do not trade on another trader's research—always double-check it with your own.
- Set at least a 3:1 reward-risk ratio. Risk only a third of what you are looking to make. Go into every trade thinking that you are going to make three times as much as you are putting in.

- Know your risk at all times.
- Always have a plan.
- Never trade more stocks than you can watch at any given moment.
- Never lose more than 10 percent of your capital in any given day.
- Never lose more than $5000 on any given trade.
- Update your trading strategy at least once a month.
- Update the stocks you trade every week.
- Never start trading a new stock before you have studied its historical charts.
- Make money every day.

THE WORLD OF DAY TRADING

Day trading has emerged as one of the hottest topics in the financial world over the last year. Day traders have been the first to capitalize on the technology behind direct access trading and have gained a lot of attention from the massive gains and losses they have amassed. While you hear stories of individuals who lost their entire life savings day trading, the truth is usually they were never trained or jumped right into day trading without any education whatsoever. You hear a lot more stories, however, about individuals making a lot of money in day trading. Some of these individuals are right out of school with little to no experience even investing, but someone or some firm has taken them under their wing and guided them through the world of day trading. Day trading is risky; there is no denying that. However, there is also an incredible opportunity for those who can afford the risk and have the ambition and discipline to succeed. This section will take you through some of the basics so that you can decide if day trading is or is not for you. Even if you already know you do not want to get into day trading, reading this section will help you understand how day traders were a major catalyst in bringing direct access trading tools into the mainstream. In addition, understanding the mentality of day traders also will help give you another angle when interpreting charts and stock patterns.

What Is Day Trading?

There is a new breed of bigwigs on Wall Street, and they are the day traders. No longer is it a prerequisite to spend years at Morgan Stanley or Goldman Sachs before you have your chance to strike it rich. Direct access trading technology has given traders the ability now to execute trades and receive data in the same way as professionals do at every Wall Street firm. This has caused numerous individuals to leave their cushy jobs with a steady paycheck to take a chance at day trading on their own. In addition, there are new players emerging who have never made a single trade in their life and who are all of a sudden becoming big-time traders because of tutelage and mentoring by other day traders. Day trading is truly for everyone—if you can afford the risk and handle the discipline.

Day trading is the act of making intraday trades. Day traders look to take positions from which they hope to make a profit in a relatively short period of time. Day traders usually are trading larger blocks of shares, in the hundred blocks, so that even with a $\frac{1}{8}$ point gain they can make several hundred dollars. However, the opposite also can be true, so it is very important for day traders to be extremely disciplined with respect to entering and exiting trades so that they are not overexposed at any point. Day traders go both long and short on stocks, but the majority tend to go long because it limits their downside risk. Day traders trade mostly stocks on the Nasdaq and look very closely at stocks that have a high number of shares being traded and are thus very liquid. This ensures their ability to quickly enter and exit trades because there is always another person on another end willing to take the opposite side of a trade. Day traders can execute their trades in a number of ways, but they mostly do so nowadays through ECNs. Because there are now a variety of ECNs, day traders employ technology that scans the multiple ECNs to find the best price possible. Although day trading has been touted by many publications as extremely risky, it does not have to be so if you are extremely disciplined and get the proper training. The number one reason people fail at day trading is that they do not approach it as a profession. Rather, they sit down once a month and "play" with it instead of devoting the proper time and seeking the right guidance to really capitalize on it.

Who Is It For?
Day trading can be for anyone, regardless of past experience with the financial markets. However, even if you have been a financial wiz for the last 20 years, it still may not be for you. Day traders need to feel comfortable with risk. This is not to say that there are ways to mitigate your risk, because there definitely are, but there is always some level of inherent risk. In addition, day traders need to be extremely disciplined. If

you cannot be 100 percent disciplined at all times, you should not get into day trading. The temptation is too great and too frequent to be undisciplined. Too many traders have lost their shirts because they were "100 percent positive" on a given trade and just risked too much. The most successful day traders are the ones who have been around the longest. They have adopted their strategies over time, and they have been able to stick to their discipline goals. And do not think that you cannot make money if you are disciplined. Any one who wants to get into day trading should allow themselves at least 3 to 6 months of not making any money. Any individual who gets into day trading expecting to make millions in their first 6 months is doomed to failure. Those who are the most successful are the ones who start out small and gradually increase the amount they trade over time.

Day traders come from all backgrounds. Some are recently graduated college students, others may have been doctors or lawyers, and then there are also Wall Street professionals who are tired of making money for someone else. Day traders truly do come from all walks of life. The world of day trading is wide open. Anyone can get into it if he or she has the capital and the willingness to learn. Those who have lost a lot of money are the ones who have set out the numerous misconceptions about day trading that currently exist in the marketplace. The truth is that day trading is risky, but it is not as risky as you might think if you are disciplined and have a conservative trading style. Day trading is just like any other profession, but you are the boss, which makes it a little more or less risky depending on how you look at it. Thus, even if off the top of your head you may not think it is for you, read on and learn a bit more about the world of day trading.

How Well Can You Do?

The sky is truly the limit. Some day traders make tens of millions of dollars a year, whereas others make $100,000. As a day trader, you are in many ways an entrepreneur. How well you do directly corresponds with how much money you make. It is important to note that even though a select group of people is making in the millions every year, these individuals are usually taking on a greater amount of risk to get to this level as well. There are many day traders who take home a very nice six-figure salary year in and out and take very little risk in the marketplace. They are extremely disciplined individuals who have carefully refined their strategies year after year. You are the boss as a day trader. You can

set your own hours, work as hard as you choose, and take days off whenever you like. But remember, the most important thing as a day trader is
to treat it as a profession, the most important job in the world. The most
successful day traders never take days off because they love what they
do so much and they cannot stand the fact that they may miss out on an
opportunity on any given day.

You always hear day traders talking about their *capital base*. This
means the amount of money they have to trade with in the markets. The
larger your capital base, the more money you have to trade with in the
markets, and the more money you can make. However, just because you
may have a million dollars of capital does not mean that you can turn
that into $10 million. The key once again is using discipline and setting
goals for yourself. Many day traders take money out of their accounts as
they generally build up their capital base and use it for other things. They
have their trading accounts, and then they have their "other money" that
they may use to make longer-term investments or just to have as cash.
The one thing that is for certain is that every day trader has his or her
own way of doing things. From trading strategy to discipline rules to
everything else, every day trader will give you a different answer.
Therefore, it is up to you to take in everything around you and come up
with a set of guidelines for yourself.

Risks

Becoming a day trader definitely has its risks. There is almost always a
period of time in the beginning when it is very difficult to make any
money at all. Although this can vary from 1 week to 6 months, with some
people never getting it at all, you need to be aware of the risks before-
hand. The biggest risk to a day trader is actually himself or herself.
Discipline is so important that you must be able to set strict guidelines
for yourself or you are doomed to failure. Although your guidelines un-
doubtedly will change over time, they need to be second nature to you
as you are trading so that you can make split-second decisions without
giving them any thought. There are also capital risks for day traders. You
usually do need anywhere from $10,000 to $25,000 to get into day trading. Although numerous individuals borrow money to begin day trading,
these also carry their own independent risks. Some day trading firms will
even allow their traders to trade on a 2:1 margin. There is also market
risk that every day trader deals with on a daily basis. The markets are
changing every day, and it is important for day traders to be able to

recognize this and update their strategy. Just because you may be making a killing for 2 weeks does not guarantee that you will do the same over the next 2 weeks. Every day the market changes. It is up to you to be able to recognize what has changed and update your strategy accordingly. The most successful day traders are the ones who can recognize the market changes and adapt their strategies accordingly. Especially, for example, when the market tanks, day traders often come in "licking their chops" the following day hoping to find bargain stocks on which they can make money. Although day traders undertake numerous risks, they do so because there are incredible rewards possible as well. Trading hours are from 9:30 A.M. to 4:30 P.M., and although these are an incredibly intense 7 hours, it beats 12-hour days (however, in the beginning especially, you should be spending time outside market hours studying your trades and talking to other traders). In addition, where else can you make your own rules and make as much money as you possibly can with no one holding you back. Although the risks to day trading are many, the rewards far outweigh them for successful day traders. The key is being aware of them from the beginning and being disciplined enough to never be overexposed.

Discipline

Discipline is the number one friend or enemy of the day trader. Talk to any number of successful day traders, and they will almost always tell you that the most important thing to remain focused on is discipline. Direct access trading tools are very powerful, and anyone using them, but especially day traders, needs to have an extraordinary amount of discipline to trade. The reason is that there is really no sort of safety net to direct access trading. You hit one button, and funds have been exchanged and a trade executed. This leaves little room for "impulse buys" or putting too much on the line in any one trade. The reason discipline is so critical, even more so than for other direct access traders, is that day traders are forced to make split-second decisions. Therefore, in many cases they have very little time to actually examine a trade and refer to their goals and checklists. For day traders, this sort of information needs to be second nature. They need to be able to make split-second decisions without having to think if they "really should or should not" make any given trade. For this to happen, their goals and discipline must be permanently ingrained in their heads. There is so little margin for error as a day trader. Any impulses to trade more shares than you should or to get into a stock blindly that you know nothing about can ruin an entire month of work. Some of the best day traders make daily goals for themselves of how much money they want to make. Whether it is $500 or $5000, each day they follow their goals in order to achieve that level. Random or impulse buys can wipe this out in no time and set a dangerous precedent for the future.

Discipline is so important for day traders, and not just in following strict guidelines (imposed on yourself) when you are trading. Especially when you are first starting out, it is very important to spend time before and after the market closes examining your trades and talking with other traders. This is the best way to begin getting comfortable with your day trading strategy. Although you should not take everything to heart that other day traders tell you, they are often an excellent source of information in providing another viewpoint on a given topic or pointing you in the right direction for a particular stock that has been active. It also takes discipline after you have had a particularly good or bad day to continue working after 4:30 P.M. to try to hone in on what you did so well or so poorly. Being disciplined also means setting daily, monthly, and annual goals for yourself. Day trading is not for everyone, and it is important that you measure your results against these goals to make sure that you are going where you want to go. Discipline comes in many ways, shapes, and forms for the day trader. The one aspect that is consistent throughout is that without discipline, you will not succeed as a day trader.

The Day Trader Psyche

Each day trader has an individual psyche. An individual's trading psyche usually depends in large part on his or her trading style and the goals he or she has set. While some day traders are looking to hit home runs (although this is not a recipe for prolonged success as a day trader), others are looking to make consistent gains day in and day out. These "consistent gainers" are the ones you should model yourself after if you want to make it as a day trader. As mentioned earlier, the markets are changing every day, and there are so many things that cause stocks to move up and down that it is impossible to always be right. Therefore, you are definitely going to be making losing trades—get ready for it. Even the most successful day traders are maybe making 60 to 70 percent successful trades. Plenty of other day traders who make in the six figures every year are making fewer than 50 percent successful trades day in and day out. However, there is a reason they are still making so much money throughout the course of the year. First of all, their winner trades obviously outdo their losing trades. Second, they are not looking to hit home runs. If you are consistently making individual trades anywhere in the double-digit range of your total trading capital, you can be out of day trading very quickly or at least wipe out months of profit on a single trade. Making sure you start with a trading psyche that is geared more toward hitting singles than home runs is a very good way to make sure you give yourself the proper foundation to build your trading capital. Everyone has a trading psyche that develops and changes over time, but having the wrong type of expectations when you get into day trading can be dangerous. Those who understand this will take a couple of months to learn the fundamentals and then start out small and try to grow every month—this offers the best chance for success.

Tools

The tools for day traders are exactly the same tools that any direct access trader uses. The main difference for day traders is that if you are thinking of day trading as a profession, you should seriously consider going to an actual day trading firm. Day trading firms are able to simulate the environment of an actual trading floor, which for most people represents a better trading environment. There are other traders to talk to, there are televisions and other data sources dispersed throughout the offices, day trading firms usually have the best computers and fastest online connections, and most day trading firms also provide you with the back end to monitor your profits and losses and provide other basic bookkeeping functions. As a day trader, you need to have the best tools. Because speed is of the utmost importance, even a slight delay of a couple of seconds due to a slower system can result in losing significant amounts of money. Therefore, it also becomes very important to do your own homework on the different day trading firms in deciding which one has the best tools, best environment, and most reliable systems. This is usually fairly easy to find out—just talk to a group of traders (and ex-traders) from any given firm to get a sense.

How Hard Is It to Become a Day Trader?

Becoming a day trader is not easy. Throw any ideas of making millions in your first month right out the window. Day trading is very different from any other sort of direct access trading. Where numerous individuals use direct access trading for longer-term trades or to get in on a particular initial public offering, day traders are really competing with other professional traders. This is the case because day traders rely primarily on technical analysis to make decisions on where a stock will move in the next hour, minute, or even 10 seconds. Longer-term direct access traders usually are looking much closer at the fundamental analysis of the company and are hoping for a gain over the long term (although they obviously would not mind if the stock spiked in the short term). Therefore, longer-term direct access traders are competing more with normal investors, over whom they have a significant edge using direct access trading tools, whereas day traders are competing with other professional traders. All this means is that it takes longer for a day trader to get his or her skills to where they need to be to compete with the professionals. It also means that you need to have a different set of expectations getting into it and a longer time period of education to master the fundamentals.

So, is it hard to become a day trader? Yes. Can anyone do it, regardless of their background? Yes again. It just takes time and commitment to learn, like anything else. Remember, if day trading were so easy, everyone would be doing it. However, many of the people who fail did not have the proper guidance, expectations, and discipline to succeed. Many people just jumped into day trading when they heard it was a way to make a killing in the markets, half expecting to make millions right off the bat. Learning to become a successful day trader takes time, but the rewards are definitely worth it for those who succeed.

Love of the Markets
Any one who gets into day trading needs to be interested in the financial markets. It is not necessary to have a financial or investment background, but you need to be intrigued by the markets and look forward to studying them. The most successful day traders hate to take days off because they feel as if they are going to miss out on a great opportunity in the markets. Day traders do not get into day trading because they may only have to work from 9:30 A.M. to 4:30 P.M. They do so because they are intrigued by the financial markets, enjoy the fast-paced nature of trading, and want to make money. Take some time before you get into day trading to make sure that you are interested in the financial markets. Also make sure that you are comfortable with the fast-paced nature of trading. Although on an hourly basis your days may be shorter, they are incredibly intense hours. There is very little let-up during the course of the day where you can afford to not be focused. There is a reason trading floors have the

reputations they do—there are a lot of very intense people there all trying to make money!

How Do I Take the First Step?

The first step to doing anything is always the hardest. The same can very easily be said about day trading. Who can afford not to make any money for 3 to 6 months? Well, as we said before, day trading is not easy, and it takes a serious commitment—this is why not everyone does it. However, for those who succeed, the financial and personal rewards are amazing. So how do you know if it is for you? You need to ask yourself a couple of basic questions:

- Can I afford not to make any money for 3 to 6 months?
- Do I have the money with which to get started?
- Am I very interested in the financial markets (this does not mean do I have experience in the markets)?
- Am I comfortable with the stress of day trading?
- Am I comfortable with the risks of day trading?
- Am I disciplined enough to stick to a very defined trading strategy?
- Do I have an interest in the financial markets?

Do not be upset if you did not answer yes to all these questions. Once you get comfortable with direct access trading on a smaller level, you may find that you are ready to take the next step. It is important, however, to be very aware of all these issues before you get into day trading. Day trading is an excellent profession for those who can get into it and are able to spend the time learning how to be successful. For those who make it, it is an incredible career that often offers a very good financial reward.

So how do you take the first step if you think you really do want to do it? You get your personal house in order, so to speak. Write down your personal goals, and examine your financial situation. If everything checks out, then read more about day trading and what it takes to succeed. If you are still getting "a warm, fuzzy feeling," then the next step is to find a place where you can day trade. It is a good idea to spend a day in a number of places to get a feel for the environment and what it is actually like. This is often a great way to make sure that day trading excites you. Do not worry if you feel intimidated at these places in the beginning, but you should at least be dying to get in there and get started. If you are, then give yourself milestones and goals for once you get started. Map out a clear path containing both a good- and bad-case scenario. Remember, you really need to give yourself at least 6 months to see if it is for you. If you have started making money by this point, you should be well on your way—as long as you remain disciplined!

The Future of Day Trading

As mentioned earlier in this book, it is the technology behind day trading that makes it so exciting for everyone. Although day traders have been the early adopters of direct access technology, in the next couple of years, millions of individuals will begin using it, whether they realize it or not. Many of the large brokerage firms themselves are investing in ECNs and trying to create user interfaces that will make direct access trading much easier for anyone to do. As for day traders, they are usually the ones with the best knowledge of direct access trading tools. Therefore, they will once again be the early adopters as additional opportunities emerge for use of the technology. Most notable probably will be the ability to trade other securities more easily, such as NYSE stocks and bonds, options, and others. The power behind direct access trading is that it eliminates the "middleman." The effects are extreme given the fact that the world's financial markets historically have been plagued with more "middlemen" than most other industries. Therefore, the ramifications of new market-places such as ECNs and technologies are extremely significant. In addition, as the Internet continues to connect individuals worldwide, there could truly be a global marketplace for the first time ever. Although numerous legal issues still need to be resolved regarding overseas trading, we are not far away from a time when the technology will allow unprecedented opportunities for international investments. Day traders trade stocks that move. Many of them often do not even know the name of the company, just the stock symbol they use to punch it up, let alone anything about them. The one thing that is for sure is that as the technology advances and new opportunities are available, day traders will be the first ones there to take advantage of them.

Developing Your Approach

There are many ways to approach day trading, but as we have discussed throughout this section, the most important thing to do is to approach everything in a disciplined fashion. In large part, however, determining what types of stocks you trade as a day trader has a great deal to do with how much risk you take on. For example, when individuals start day trading, they should really stick with stocks in the $5 to $10 range. These stocks generally tend not to move as much over the course of a day and are a perfect way to get your feet wet without exposing yourself too much. More experienced day traders may only trade stocks priced at over $100 a share, in a specific sector, or stocks that they know have spiked large amounts in the past. As a general rule of thumb, the higher the share price of a stock, the more it can move over the course of a day. While this obviously does not hold true always, it is a good rule to hold onto in the beginning. Most experienced traders trade more expensive stocks; therefore, it is a good idea to start in the "minor leagues" of stocks before jumping up to this level. Anyone who starts his or her day trading career wanting to trade stocks like Amazon.com and Yahoo! is going to be in trouble. Therefore, the key becomes identifying some stocks that trade in a particular range and that trade in an industry that is not extremely volatile. For example, an Internet stock that is going public next week at $10 a share would still not be a good one to start with because the company is in the Internet industry and is just going public, two extreme indicators that the stock could spike significantly either way. Besides individual stocks, there are numerous other things that affect your approach to day trading. Most important once again is your discipline in sticking to the goals you outlined for yourself in the beginning. However, by picking the right group of stocks to start off trading with, you will make it much easier on yourself.

QUESTIONS TO ASK YOURSELF

1 Do I have enough interest in the markets to trade for a living?
2 Do I have enough capital to trade for a living?
3 Can I afford not to make any money as I learn to day trade over the next 3 to 6 months?
4 Am I comfortable with the risk I am assuming?
5 What are my personal goals as a trader?
6 Am I going to trade from home, or am I going to go to a professional trading firm?
7 How am I going to brush up on the skills I need to become a successful trader?
8 Do I know an individual or group of individuals who can help mentor me as I begin to trade for a living?

7

QUESTIONS AND ANSWERS

Q: How hard is it to master the fundamentals of direct access trading?

A: It takes time, like anything else, but the technology is out there. The key is to just make a commitment to learn the basics. You are still essentially just buying and selling stocks; you just have the tools to do so in a professional manner. The key is to really decide what you want to get out of direct access trading and then set realistic goals toward achieving it.

Q: What is so different about direct access trading?

A: Direct access trading allows you to trade with the same tools as the Wall Street professionals. As of a couple of years ago, the "walls" to the Wall Street have come tumbling down. Any individual now with the right tools can access the markets directly. This is a good thing, but no one should do it until they have spent appropriate time mastering the fundamentals—because it is very different from something like online investing. Direct access trading has gotten a lot of attention as of late because of day traders, who were the pioneers in using this technology, but it is really for anyone, and you do not have to assume the risks of a day trader to take advantage of it. With direct access trading, you have open to you a whole new set of tools and real-time market- and stock-specific information. It takes some time to learn, but is well worth it in the long run.

Q: How long will it take me to master the fundamentals?

A: It takes each individual a different amount of time to learn the basics of direct access trading. Most important, it really depends on what you want to use it for. Do you want to be a day trader? Do you want to start making all your trades this way and become a long-term direct access trader? Or do you want to become a part-time day trader? It really depends on which of these best suits your desires. However, if you want to be involved in day trading at all, it can take anywhere from 3 to 6 months to really learn the skills you need. If you want to use it to get better information and better prices, you may be able to do it in a couple of weeks. The key is to go in with your eyes wide open and realize that there is quite a bit to learn, but the good part is that anyone can learn it. You do not need a major in economics to understand what is going on. I have seen an array of people get into this that you would not even believe. And over time, everyone will be using this on some level. So you are really just getting in ahead of the curve.

Q: What are the main things I am going to need to learn?

A: The main things every new direct access trader needs to understand are market makers, electronic communication networks (ECNs), and level II quotes. In addition to these, the biggest thing is for a new direct access trader to just get comfortable with the look and feel of the trading screen. Another thing that is often overlooked but is very important is the ability to move quickly on the keyboard. In direct access trading there is no "Undo" button, and split seconds can make all the difference. This is all stuff that is not difficult to learn, but it does take a bit of time.

Q: How much more do I need to know to use direct access trading instead of my online investing account?

A: The basics are still the same—you are buying and selling stocks. What is different is how you are going about doing it. You have more tools at your disposal and better access to information—you just have to learn how to harness it. Fortunately, new companies have emerged that provide the software or Web-based application to take much of this confusion away. Therefore, you really do not need to know any more—you are just going to be required to learn a little bit more. And regardless of previous experience with the stock market, anyone can use direct access trading tools. The main difference comes when you start thinking about day trading or trading for a living—this is a very different situation and one that usually requires a full-time commitment.

Q: What are the basic things people should know up front if they are considering starting to trade for a living? What should they be aware of? What do they need to know in terms of capital, amount of time they need, general issues, etc.?

A: Well, I think that expectations should be kind of low in the beginning. The amount of information you are presented at the very beginning is just overwhelming, and the more you spend time learning in the beginning, the better trader you are going to be long term. A lot of people tend to jump in too soon because they are excited about the opportunity, but they really need to spend time learning the fundamentals first.

I personally think that to get started in direct access trading at any level, going at it one step at a time is the best way. When I teach someone, I start teaching them one skill at a time, and hopefully, they can master that skill and then move on to another. For instance, I would never have someone who is new at this start shorting stocks. I would have them only go long, with the same strategy every time, until they have mastered that skill. The key is really starting off with the basics and then moving on from there. Just realize that if you want to trade for a living, it can be a risk profession in some respects until you get the hang of it, but there are clearly steps you can take to mitigate this risk.

Q: What are the steps you can take to lessen your risk?

A: A lot of attention has been paid recently to the idea that day trading firms are too risky and that 75 percent of day traders do not make any money. I don't know what these people are doing. Maybe it is their lack of training, and training is very important, but I don't see why so many people are losing money at this. It doesn't have to be a losing proposition, so to speak. The best traders that I know did not start making $20,000 a day. Some of them may be doing it on average now, but some of them went 6 months without making a dime. Then they started making $500 a day, and then $1000 a day, and then $1500. Then one day they do $3000 and say, "Hey, that wasn't that hard; all I did was a little more of what I know how to do," and they begin to step it up.

   However, these days you see a couple people come into a very hot market where everything's flying, and they buy a thousand shares of stock and it goes up 4 points and they sell. They make $4000 on this trade, but then they make a couple of other trades where they break even, and they think they are trading experts. Unfortunately, the second a little bit of a choppy market—or even a down market—comes along, they get crushed because they buy, and they hold, and they lose money. These are individuals who just jump into it without having done their homework. You have to recognize when the market is changing and it is time to change your strategy—this only comes with experience.

Q: How do you do this? How do you adjust your strategy?

A: Talking to other people. Discussing it. "What do we think is going on? What are you guys thinking? How has the market changed?" Basically people realized you cannot buy as much stock. If the volume's dead again, you cannot buy as much stock, and you cannot give much room on the downside.

   In a raging bull market, which is what it was for 3 months, if something tanked 2 points, I'd have no problem letting it go down and buying a couple more. You could just tell that the market wanted to explode. Now, if the market changes, you cannot hold on. You are going to get hurt. So it does take sometimes a couple of days to adjust like this, but you have got to talk to other people about it, other traders. CNBC will give you the analysts, but they can find a million analysts that are bulls, and they can find a million analysts that are bears. They can just keep bringing on people until they are blue in the face. You talk to the people who are actually in there trading it, and this is why analysis is sometimes good on CNBC but not really very useful. But it is better than the other stuff as far as media goes. In any case, I would consider myself a very conservative trader; it is part of what has given me longevity.

Q: When you say you are "conservative," how do you approach trading in a conservative way?

A: To me, the most fundamental aspect of trading is risk management and risk to reward. And in my opinion, I want to set that risk to reward as high or as low—however you want to look at it—as possible. In other words, I want to risk as little as possible to make as much as possible. You ask, "All right, which are the best stocks for me to trade given my risk reward scenario?" I am basically looking to make about a 3:1 ratio when I execute a trade and only stick with stocks I am comfortable trading. Essentially, I'm looking to risk $100 to make $300 on every trade. Sometimes I'll risk $1000 to make $3000 or $500 to make $1500, but I always start out each trade with about a 3:1 ratio in mind. And depending on what I see, I'll go for a little more or take a little less.

Q: What differentiates a very conservative trader from a very aggressive one?

A: There are plenty of people who can go out there and make a couple of grand a day. Is that optimizing the situation? I think if you are only saying I'm going to make $1000 today and I'm going to get out, then you are not maximizing your chances of making a lot of money. On the days that $1000 is the only thing that's there, that's fine. When you lose $1000, you lose $1000. But if there's $10,000 out there, why would you not want to sit there and make it? That would be very conservative. That's one way to identify it.

The second is amount of shares. There are a lot of people who would say, "I'm not buying anything else. I'm not buying more." That's also conservative. If I get in a high-probability situation, I'm going to buy more. The market's going up, you're in a strong stock, and there are buyers. Maybe there was good news in the morning.

That's a high-probability situation. A high-probability situation is a strong stock on a weak day when the market starts to turn. A weak trader may buy 100 or 200 shares or even 500 shares of one stock. If I'm aggressive, I may buy 2000 shares of everything I can find. On a day like today I did, and that's why I made a lot of money. I loaded up. I maximized my buying power. I have no problem with having around $2 million in the market, but some people have a problem having more than two positions. I'll have ten; I don't care. So, in this particular case, I was more aggressive. But I wasn't aggressive without an end in sight. I knew what I wanted to do and how it could be done. So, as evidenced by my gains, it was smart and not just aggressive.

Q: When you are trading for a living, what is the sort of environment you need? What is it you need to succeed in terms of the environment?

A: Well, there are a few people who can be disciplined enough to teach themselves and push themselves. I've learned through experience that I'm not one of them. I mean, I can make a very good living by myself anywhere on the planet doing this, but I'm never going to push myself as much as if I'm in an environment with other successful people, because I'm a competitive person. And knowing that about myself, when I see one of my friends—or maybe even someone I don't know—doing better than me, it pushes me. And I don't necessarily beat myself up by saying, "Oh, that guy's better than me. What am I doing?" It's just that I might be happy making $500 or $1000 dollars a day by myself—when I'm in a vacuum to the rest of the world as opposed to saying, "You know what, there are guys making $20,000 a day, and I'm stopping at $500!" And $500 a day is a very good living, it works out to about $100,000 a year, but when you look around and see others doing very well, that's what's going to push you.

Q: Take me through what a typical trading day is like for you. I'm sure every day is a little bit different, but just describe any rituals you go through, or what you do throughout the course of the day.

A: Each day I basically have a list of stocks that I intend to follow. That list generally stays the same but slowly evolves over time.

Some stocks will come off that list, and others will be added, but there are about 15 or so stocks for which I evaluate what they did the day before and how they might react today. I make a kind of personal prediction as to what I think they are going to do. For instance, if there was a stock that got crushed yesterday for which I still like the technical indicators, I might look to trade that stock today. From about 8:45 to 9:15 A.M. I do this, and then from 9:15 to 9:30 A.M. I try to see what other stocks appear to be active. I go to a riser and faller's list and see what's hot in the morning and what they are talking about on CNBC. I don't like to just jump in, but I like to get an overall feel for the market and what is hot. Personally, I don't like to trade anything before the open unless maybe I have a position that I came in with, but I won't establish a position before the open. Some people do, and some people have had some success with it. To me, it's kind of like learning a whole new thing. I don't like anything that's unpredictable, and I feel stocks don't act as "true" before and after market hours. During the course of the day, I stay out of stocks that are too volatile. I see the possible gains in them, but if I'm viewing the risk to reward as too high, I'll stay out. Now that doesn't mean I avoid all volatile stocks; for example, if a stock is up 20 points on solid technical trends, I might trade it, but stocks that are all over the place I try to avoid. The stocks that go up 15 and then go down 15 don't seem to have any rhyme or reason, and I tend to stay away from them. I also tend to stay away from some of the large-cap stocks such as Microsoft, Dell, and Cisco. They're just not particularly good trading stocks because it takes massive amounts of buying and selling to move their prices. So they're going to move, but not usually enough to make the kind of profit I am looking for. What's going to make Microsoft go up a point versus down a point? I've got no idea. So why am I going to try to make a point in Microsoft? I like to find stocks that have a direction and basically buy them on the pullbacks.

Q: Over the course of a day, are you monitoring your 15 or so stocks and looking for good opportunities to get in?

A: I am continually typing up the same stocks over and over and looking at their intraday charts. Basically, I'm looking for support levels and resistance levels. And when the stock is trading within a range that I am comfortable with, I place a couple of trades and try to make a little bit of money within that range. And when it breaks out of a range, up or down, I'll respond accordingly. Let's say I think a stock is very strong, it's been strong for days, and it's one of the stocks I've been following, so I know it pretty well. Let's say it's been trading between 74 and 76. I may look to buy or sell 100 shares in the 74 range and sell in the 76 range, but when I see a breakout above 76, I'm buying as much as I can get my hands on. Now, if it stops right there and doesn't continue, I'm pretty much selling as fast as I can. What I'm looking for that stock to do is go to 77 or 78, and that is when I make my biggest trades. On the other side, I really don't short at all. If the other side of it broke down below 74, I would start intensely watching it for a bottom. Almost every one of the stocks that I have on my list is there because I consider it to be a strong stock. I like stocks that are trending up over at least a 30-day period. So, if it breaks down below 74, I'm going to start testing it by throwing in bids. But when I see it start to slow down—in other words, more market makers are on the bid or there's more size of stock at the bid—I'm going to start to put in bids to see if people are going to sell to me.

Q: What do you do at the end of the day? Do you do anything when the markets close in terms of looking at previous trades or planning ahead for the next day?

A: I immediately write down my profit or loss, how many tickets I wrote, my average gain, and my basic information so that I have a personal record of my trading activity. I like to have my own personal information, although a lot of systems do parts of this for you. I like to do it myself just in case there's any discrepancy. I also write down any stock on which I made over $500 dollars and any stock on which I lost over $500 dollars. On the losers, I basically try to figure out why I lost it. I usually know right away after the trade, but I just try to refresh my memory as to why I lost money on that stock. On my winners, I try to remember what I did right so that next time I can take advantage of it as well and maybe even do better. I also look to see if there are any stocks that weren't a part of my list that were very active, and I potentially add them. Also, if there are any stocks on my list that have been down for 3 or 4 days that I really haven't done any trades in, I temporarily may remove them from my list.

Q: We have talked a lot about the intraday trading, but do you trade any stocks for the long term? Is this something that you recommend to people from a risk standpoint? How do you go about rounding out your portfolio?

A: Basically, when I've got a feeling on a stock, I trade it in my trading account. If I've got a feeling, or I've gotten good advice, or I just want to hold a stock for longer, I get it out of my trading account. Therefore, I am really able to differentiate the two accounts. Most people don't realize how volatile certain stocks are. Even the best-performing stock has its down days, and I may just get too tempted to sell it if it is in my trading account. So I do have other accounts that I hold stocks in, and I look at them on a day-to-day basis. But for the most part, as a professional trader, I separate it. I've got my own investments, and I may not be the best portfolio manager, so to speak, but I'm a good trader. And I know how to make money trading, so if I'm going to hold something long term, I get it out of my trading account.

Q: What does it take, monetarily, to get started if you want to trade for a living?

A: You really can't expect to make money your first 3 months at a minimum, and it can take up to 6 months for some people. But I don't think that means you have to lose money, and once you get over the hump, you can make up for the difference very quickly. So you do have to be in a financial position that you can afford to have no income for that 6-month period. As far as capital that you need, I don't think it takes that much. The reason I say this is because in today's market there is a stock every day that's up 20 points. If you look at any given risers and fallers list recently, there usually are 45 stocks that are up more than 10 points. That's a lot of stocks to trade that are moving very quickly. And although a lot of them are over $100 or $200, there are a lot of them that are under $200 as well. So for any stock under $200, a hundred shares at a time, with a margin of 2:1—you only need $10,000 to trade. So I personally think you can get started in this with $10,000, margin 2:1. In the beginning you shouldn't be trading more than one stock at a time anyway, and that gives you enough money to trade the one stock at a time and get to learn the business. And if you buy a hundred shares of stock and it goes 2 points, that's $200. Basically you look to make a point here, a point there—and eventually you step it up. You start buying 200 shares or start trying to curb your losses a little bit more. But in terms of capital requirements, I think you can get started on $10,000 if you can afford to go the 6 months without making money.

Q: What type of background do you need to be a good direct access trader?

A: I've seen a lot of different types of people do this and be successful at it. I don't think it's so much of a background that's required as a few personality traits. I think you can come from all walks of life, get into this, and be successful. Anyone that I can think of, if they spend the right amount of time mastering the fundamentals, can at least use direct access trading on some level.

Q: What are the characteristics, the attributes, it helps to have to become a successful direct access trader?

A: A certain aspect of entrepreneurship helps, because you are your own business, especially if you are looking to do this for a living. You really need to push yourself to always be learning more and doing better. You also need a certain level of responsibility because there are a lot of new things to learn. It takes time to master the fundamentals, but you've got to be willing to put in the effort. It also really helps to have a competitive spirit.

Q: How do you continue learning over time to keep becoming a more successful trader?

A: It's kind of an industry of patterns. Like the saying in the industry goes, "Past performance is not indicative of future results." However, things tend to repeat themselves. This is where experience helps so much, because once you've seen it one time, you can make a calculated judgment as to whether scenario A, B, or C is going to happen this time. And that's basically what I do when I trade. I analyze what's happening at the moment and compare it with my own personal database of all the things I've seen and say, "Based on that, I think this is going to happen." The same types of patterns repeat over and over and over. There are times that the market doesn't do what you expect, and that's where your true test of being a good trader comes into play. The key is not to let emotions get involved. Like I said before, I sometimes limit my upside because I limit my downside. If a stock is not doing exactly what I was expecting, I'm done with it and will sell the position. And a lot of times, it'll very shortly after do exactly what I thought it was going to do, but I'd rather do that than have it go against me and lose $500, $1000, $5000, whatever it might be. Basically, I'm a sore loser, and I try to have as few losing trades as possible.

That's another thing you have to realize as a trader. You have to realize that you are going to have losing trades. It's a question of how bad those losses are because you are going to have winning trades too. And your winners don't necessarily have to be more than your losers—in terms of number—but you've got to make more money on your positive trades versus your losing trades.

Q: Why is it that individuals do not make it as successful traders? What happens to most people who do not make it?

A: Fortunately, I've never been in that situation, so I can't really speak firsthand. All I can really talk about is what I've seen. People get stubborn, and some of the biggest losses that I've seen were over pure stubbornness. Some people get incredibly aggressive with their newfound tools and start to average down a position, and then the unexpected happens, and it becomes an enormous loss that they can't deal with. Other people—it's an emotional game; it's almost like a professional athlete who lets his mind frame get in the way. Keeping a positive mental frame is important. When you see someone get into that negative frame of mind, they start to go downhill.

Q: What has changed over the last couple of years that has made the trading environment different? How different is trading than a couple of years ago?

A: ECNs are probably the biggest difference, because of what they enable the direct access trader to do. They didn't exist when I first started trading, and they've brought a lot of liquidity to the market, but they've also made it a little bit trickier. However, my strategy has always really been the same and will continue to be so. I limit my losses before I look to reap huge gains. Other people will disagree. I've been in a lot of seminars and heard a lot of other people talk about how you have to run with your winners, and that's some-what true. I mean, you don't want to continually sell your good trades and your good positions and then hold onto your losers. The conservative approach limits my upsides somewhat but protects my downside. Therefore, I tend to make money no matter what the market's doing.

Q: In terms of volatility and sheer volume, what effects have things like ECNs had on trading?

A: They have made it much better. For the better traders, they're making more money than ever before. I mean, the fact that the top 50 stocks are moving 10 points or better—or 5 points or better—for the day traders who are getting involved in these stocks, and really know the ins and outs of these stocks, it's a huge moneymaker. For those longer-term direct access traders, the opportunities are still fantastic because the market has been doing so well in general.

Q: What about people who are just getting into direct access trading? Is it a good time for them to get into it?

A: It's bad if they don't realize that the market cannot go up forever. If they think, "All right, there's a stock up 20 points every day, so why don't I just buy a thousand shares of that stock, and I'll make a killing." However, if you go over to the other side, their stock's down 20 points every day as well. You can really get hurt quickly if your eyes are too big for your plate, so to speak. So that's why I believe in starting slow, regardless of how active you are planning on being. Learn to be positive. For example, if you think you might be interested in trading for a living, write 10 tickets a day without losing money. Then learn to write 10 tickets a day when making some money. Then learn to write 20 tickets a day when making some money. Then try to make $500 every day. Then try to do $1000. Some people will stay at $1000 longer than others, but when you can do it consistently, look to push yourself again, no matter how high you get . . . and then continue to push yourself, no matter how high you get, continue to push yourself. The key is to set re-alistic goals, at any level, and continue to push yourself to do better and to understand the markets better.

Q: What are the traits you have to have to keep improving as a trader and to maintain your edge year after year when the markets are changing?

A: Just keep doing it, and stay persistent. Focus on the markets every day on some level. The longer you are away from the market, the more it's going to change, and the harder it will be to catch up, so to speak. You don't even realize that you're evolving as the market evolves. It goes back to trying to trade for a living doing $500 a day and then trying to do $1000 a day. It's obviously going to be easier to do it in some markets than in other markets, and sometimes you need to take a step back. You can get up to a point where you're doing $5000 every day and it's easy. Then the market changes, and all of a sudden, you're losing money. So what you've got to do is start over. Say, if you've lost money for 3 days in a row, you should set your goal at being positive again. And then, the next day set your goal at $500 or $1000. And then, the next day—until you can learn what's going on in today's marketplace and can catch back up to your overall goal. There have been times—and there's been at least 50 times in the 5 years—that I've been trading, that I sort of hit the reset button, and have said, "All right, whatever I'm doing isn't working, so let's start over and try some different things."

Q: Now one of the things you have mentioned before is you have seen so much change, such as ECNs evolving. How has this changed in terms of the tools you really need to trade? There are obviously different levels of tools that people use to trade. Some people are trying to use their Ameritrade account at home, while others are actually in a trading firm using the best technology available. What are the tools you really need to be on par with the best?

A: I would say that anybody who's not using a direct access system—looking at level II quotes with access to all the ECNs—is not using the best tools available in the marketplace. There's just no way they could keep up with anyone else in doing that. It's not to say they couldn't make money, but if they're making money, sitting at home on Ameritrade, they'd be making ten times that on a level II system. They'd also be amazed at how much information they're missing.

Q: How is the information different when you are using direct access trading tools?

A: I know most of the online brokers provide snapshot quotes. If you're getting a snapshot quote, you're not even seeing the current market price, and most people don't realize how quickly that market price is changing. Everyone reading this book should know that if they really want to take advantage of direct access, they are crazy not to trade with active quotes. In addition, the data feeds with fundamental news and technical analysis are unparalleled.

So, getting instant quotes is crucial, and one of the things that changes this is ECNs. ECNs are very active on the inside market— the highest bid and lowest offer. Now, for the regular person out there, I know that the software company Tradescape has a product coming out that's going to be very good. But I think that for someone who's not a professional day trader or looking to become one, it would be a little bit of information overload. However, these people are designing new technology that everybody's going to be using, even people who aren't day traders, so my guess is that it will soon be easy to use for all involved. I mean, how would anyone ever buy stock if you buy it and then have to wait 2 seconds, only to see that by that time the price changed? So it's important to say that anyone doing more than 10 trades a day should have direct access because that means they're sitting there looking at the market on a daily basis. And I don't necessarily mean 10,000 shares. I mean, 10 trades. It could be 1000 shares total of a 100 shares a piece. The point is to give them better prices based on automatically routing them to the best price at the current market price.

Q: What are the different trading styles you see people using?

A: This weekend at a trade show I sat in on a panel that was the "Secrets of the Top 1 Percent of Direct Access Traders," and I listened to some of the questions that were asked from the audience. A woman got up, and she was very angry because she felt they were not disclosing any secrets. She screamed at them, "This is supposed to be a seminar on the *secrets* of the top 1 percent, so I want to hear some secrets now." The panel members were all responding, "We're not keeping anything from you—there are no secrets to this." But as far as styles go, "in and out" is probably the most pure form of day trading. Basically, it's making spreads, is one way to term it, or in and out. And you're basically paying the offer for a stock for which the spread tells you it's about to run. You buy the stock as it's going up, you throw it up on the offer, and you sell it when it starts to slow down or the spread starts to widen.

Q: Is this the kind of main other approach that people use?

A: There's making the spread, in and out, and I don't know what you would call what I do. I guess you could call it relative strength or something like that. I know there's an actual term that means that, and I don't think it's exactly the same thing. But that's playing the strongest stocks when the market's going to go up. There's definitely different stuff. There's bottom fishing, which I personally don't do because I feel there isn't as much upside potential for bottom fishing.

Q: By bottom fishing, you mean . . . ?

A: Finding a bottom of a stock—a bottom of a down move. Usually when you refer to bottom fishing you're talking about stocks that are really getting killed, really getting smoked.

There are plenty of people who do this. It's a much more disciplined type of game. You really need to have a lot of discipline to be able to do that, and you've got to pick your spots very carefully. But if you do end up being correct, you can make a lot of money.

The reason I don't do it is because I don't feel there's as much upside to playing the long side of a weak stock. I find there's more upside playing a weak stock short. The market keeps going down, the market is going to tank a point or a point and a half, it's going to bounce maybe ⅜ of a point, and that's where I'm looking to get short. Then I'm getting short and watching it make new lows. Then watching it make new lows, getting short more, whatever.

Like I said, I play long a lot more, and I do the exact same strategy long. Stock runs up, makes a high, and I try to sell some at the high. Sometimes I'll hold a core position, let it come back down a little bit, and then throw in a bid. If my bid doesn't get hit, I'll pay the offer, and I'll pay through the offer if I think it's going to keep going up. Then the stock makes new highs. Once a stock cracks high, it's going to hopefully keep running a bit if it has the momentum, if it was near its high when it started the move. Of course, sometimes a stock bounces off its highs, and then you either sell some of the other highs or you hold on and wait for it to come back.

Q: Tell me why you trade so much more long than you do short?

A: Just more upside. I'm definitely all about high-probability situations. I don't do anything mathematical, but it's like blackjack. You can't win if you don't double down, and I just really feel if the cards are right at that time, that's a situation you want to be in. So it's kind of like would you play blackjack at a one-deck table or a four-deck table? You've got much better odds at the one-deck table because it's easier to read what's going on. I'm not saying it's easier to read, but the market goes up more than it goes down. And if that changes, I'm not opposed to playing short more at all. Not one bit. Today I was loaded short in a whole bunch of stocks. In some cases it worked; in some cases it didn't. But in both cases it allowed me to see which stocks were strong at that point. If they weren't going down and I was short, I would know to get long on the next up move, or if they were tanking, I would know what was weak, and I was making money.

Q: It sounds like what you are saying is that trading style is a very individual thing. I mean, you really develop your own strategy over time. But what does it take to get to a level where you can do it? I mean, for some people, I'm sure it is better keeping a conservative approach over time.

A: I hate comparing this to gambling because it is not. However, this example will illustrate the point very well. In blackjack, if you're dealt a 5 and a 6 and you've got a $5 bet, and the dealer's got a 6 showing, you double down. It's what the rules tell you to do. But if you've got a $10,000 bet and the same cards come out, you might think about it only because of the money. You shouldn't, but hypothetically, let's just say it makes you uncomfortable. You don't know why you bet that, or it was everything you had. Should you borrow the money to double down when you know it's the right thing to do? No, because what it means is that you're playing at a level you're not comfortable with. So whether you're conservative or aggressive, I think that anyone who you would deem as aggressive, I'd call more experienced because they didn't start that way. Anyone who starts this way is going to get killed.

Q: How did you come up with your trading strategy?

A: It was a combination. I think the most important thing is being around experienced traders and just asking questions all the time.

Constantly. Just hammering people for information. For example, if I saw that somebody had a great day and I saw that it was some stock that I was in, I would go and ask the person what he or she had done and how he or she had made money. So it's all about asking questions and being around good traders.

Q: What do you think other people should look at when they are examining their own trading strategy?

A: I never really planned on developing it or anything like that—it just kind of came along. I've never really sat there and analyzed it. I have a few fundamental things that I go by, such as if I'm trading stocks long, I play the strongest stocks, and if I'm playing stuff short, I play the weakest stocks. That's the absolute most important thing, I think. Another fundamental rule I live by is if I get myself into a high-probability situation, I really try to take advantage of it.

Q: Have you found that your strategy and what you have been doing has changed since you started?

A: Absolutely. At first, when I started to get decent, I was watching about 10 stocks that people call their "bread and butter" stocks. So that was my strategy at the beginning—know the stocks, know the market makers. Now I have gotten to the point where I can trade any stock because I can always equate it to some other stock that I've traded in the past.

Q: How hard is it to get to know your stocks? Do you try to remember what they do over time?

A: Yes. There are Web sites you can look at, including the Nasdaq Trader Web site, that tell you who does all the volume in the stocks. They don't tell you if the person is a buyer or a seller, but they tell you who the big players are. That's one way to find out information. Another way is just by watching. I've heard people say that they would type up a stock and they wouldn't even plan on making money in a stock the first 5 or 10 trades they'd make, and they'd just write a bunch of tickets so they could see who was buying and who was selling. You've obviously got to be careful what kind of stock you're doing that in, but your intent is always to make money.

Q: You have talked a lot about market makers. What are market makers, and how important is it to understand their motivating factors when you are watching a certain stock you are in?

A: Market makers are market participants who are ready to provide liquidity, or essentially to buy and sell stocks from traders. These are the people like Goldman Sachs, Merrill Lynch, and J. P. Morgan. It's tough to know their motivations. A lot of the time we kind of guess that they might be on the bid for 100 shares, but they might be in the Instinet selling on the offer. So it's very difficult to tell. But by trading you really kind of know what's going on with the stock. You'll be able to see who the actual buyers are and who the sellers are, and this helps. I think the market makers decide where the stock's going to go. It's important to watch where they are placing themselves, if they are buying or selling.

Q: How do you measure your success as a professional trader? There is obviously the easy answer (i.e., money), but what are the other things you monitor?

A: It's a very monetarily oriented profession, but I think that after awhile it's not about money anymore. It's more about numbers on my screen, where I'm trying to do better every day, week, and month. You've got to step back every once in a while, regardless of how active a trader you are, and measure it on the bigger scale. I also set a goal every month, and every time I reach that goal, I set a higher goal. I measure success by seeing the overall numbers go up. I then measure my success based on how I am doing in comparison to that and always make sure to push myself to never be complacent.

Q: How important is discipline when you are trading?

A: It's everything. You must stick to the fundamental rules that you set, even though everyone sets them differently and they are consistently changing over time. There are no rules set in stone. You don't say, "All right, Trader A joins the bid, so it's a buy, and if it gets to here, then sell." For example, I generally never have a stock that I lose more than $1000 in when I day trade. Also, I like to go back at the end of a week or a month and take a look at stocks that I'm making a lot of trades in but not really making any money in. These are the ones that become your pet stocks, that you think you're making money in, but you're not. One of my most important rules, which is very hard to do, is to stop trading a stock like that, at least for a little while. You don't have it. You're not reading it well. So move on to other stocks. Also, find the stocks that you are making money in and trade them a little heavier. You can't analyze this on a day-to-day basis. But when you get to the end of a week or a month, you can really see which stocks you're not really doing well in and which stocks you are.

Q: Do you find that when you are doing excessively well or even if you are doing poorly, your trading strategy starts to change a little bit? Like you get a little bit more aggressive or a little bit more conservative?

A: I would say yes, a little bit more aggressive. Most of the time it seems to work out. The reason is that a lot of the time when you lose money in something, it's not that you should double down or anything like that, or average down. But if something tanks fast enough that you just got cremated in it, then the chances are there's going to be an opportunity to make some of your money back—most of it, in a lot of cases, by either buying another one or hitting it out and buying it back cheaper, and then riding the outmove up.

Q: Do you think it is important to go back and analyze your losing trades at the end of the day?

A: Sure. You should always be keeping some sort of rules in your head so that you don't do the same thing again. That's when you get mad—when you do the same thing twice or something like that. In the beginning a lot of the time you're losing because of mental errors. You're buying stock in the wrong box, or on TradeScape Pro maybe you click the wrong button or something like that. That's a mental error. They're going to go away after awhile. Those aren't a big deal. Or you buy 1000 shares of the stock when you meant to buy 100. That probably happens a lot more. People forget to change the tier size. Going back and analyzing your trades, obviously you want to do that. Forget about just your losing trades or whatever—you should be paying attention to your winning trades too. I think that's just as important. And just trading rules in general, you should be keeping track of. Don't get short when the market opens down.

For instance, one of my trainees today got short when the market opened down 106 points. I just yelled at him. I couldn't believe it. You wait, and even if the market starts to attack, you're still dead if you're already down 100 right on the open, and we were smoked yesterday and the day before. You really want to be careful getting short right at that point. The market rallied right in the open, so he got in trouble.

Even if I was the guy sitting next sitting to him, or it was my friend on TradeScape Pro doing it, I'd want to know that information anyway. So I think you want to just keep asking questions and writing a list of trading rules based on your good trades, bad trades, and just things you've heard.

Q: When you hit a losing streak in a stock, how do you handle it? Do you just not trade it?

A: That's exactly how I handle it. Personally, I like to step away from it, although that's not to say I won't go back to it. But by stepping away, sometimes you get a clearer picture of why you are not making any money in it. A lot of times individuals continue to trade these stocks, but when they sit down and do the analysis of which stocks they are making money in and which ones they are not, they don't even realize it. So, when you have the discipline to go over your numbers and see what occurs, it can change the way you trade particular stocks, which can very easily be the difference between success and failure, especially if you want to eventually trade for a living.

Q: How do you get over the fear of losing money and approach it more on a numbers basis instead of thinking about every nickel and dime you make or lose?

A: It definitely comes with experience. As I was saying before, I worry more when I am really fluctuating between making and losing money and not just making steady gains. For example, if I'm down $2000, I can rationalize it and say, "Let's get back in there and make some money and make some smart trades and do it one at a time instead of trying to go for the big score." However, sometimes fear comes into me when I'm up money because I am afraid to lose it. It's really a mental game. How do you cope with that? Everyone's going to cope with it a different way, and what's important about it is that you do cope with it. You have to separate yourself from it. It is just numbers. It is just odds. If you're right a certain percentage of times—you could flip a coin a hundred times, and it could be heads a hundred times, but eventually, the odds are going to even out. And you have to keep telling yourself that. Just because you hit a bad streak of trades, you've got to keep that positive frame of mind. Say, "I'm going to take what I've learned and make smart trades." It's the kind of the trader who tries to get it all back in one shot who is destined to fail.

Q: Did you ever think that maybe direct access trading was not for you as a career?

A: I have done it for a long time now and have gone through times when I felt like I could do it forever and then other times when I didn't. But I approach it like any other job—you're going to have your ups and downs. Sometimes you're going to love your career, and sometimes you're going to hate it. I don't think it's fair to put an overall stigma on trading and say, "You can do it for 30 years" or "You're going to burn out." I don't know. Look, if I worked on an assembly line, I probably wouldn't last 5 months. But the same thing may be true if I were to be an executive of a company. It's really an individual thing for everybody, and it also depends on how active they want to become. I've chosen to become a full-time day trader, so I approach it as a career and treat it with respect and approach it very seriously.

Q: Do you think it was inherent in you that you were to become a great trader, or is it something you have really taught yourself and studied in different ways over the years? Are these sorts of skills something that can be learned?

A: I think trading is something that is learned. There are people who pick it up quicker than others, but it has to be learned. Nobody just knows how to trade. Are some people better at it than others? Yes, in some respects, but it needs to be learned just like any other skill. It also depends on how active a trader you want to become. But the bottom line is that anyone can get into it, regardless of their background, and use it to make better trades on some level.

Q: What has been your best resource in learning trading skills and becoming a better trader?

A: I personally think that other traders are your best resource. That's part of why I say being in a trading environment can be so great. Learning from experience, especially other people's experience, is everything. Eventually, over time, you can develop your own experience. Like I said before, those times that I hit the "reset" button, that's relying on my own experience. No one else is telling me hit that "reset" button. I've got to tell myself that. But I've been there enough times to know when and how to do that. For anybody new, it is probably most important to have a love for the markets and enjoy the fast-paced nature of trading. I'm fascinated with both, and that's what continues to push me. You will find that most traders can talk to you forever about it. So, in terms of learning, just talk to every trader you can. You're going to talk to some people and disagree with them completely. And you're going to talk to others and think, "That's exactly my thinking." So if you find a successful trader that's got exactly your thinking, you should try to learn everything you can from him or her, and this could mean just watching him or her or establishing a phone relationship with him or her. I know people who sit around me who are on the phone all day long talking to people. Talking to their friends who trade in other offices or remotely. But one of the things that I think has been one of the biggest aspects of my success—and that of the people around me—is communication with other traders. There's an old saying in trading: "If one person can watch 100 stocks and another person can watch 100 stocks, then two people together can watch 200 stocks." And it makes sense because if you're helping one another, it just makes you both better. That's part of the reason I commute into the city everyday to be in an office with other traders. I want to be in an environment where people are going to shout out stocks and talk about them and express their feelings on them. Although I don't always agree with my peers, and they're not always right, it is still very helpful.

Q: There is a lot of market news available, probably more than is even necessary. What sort of pieces of news do you think people can ignore?

A: If you're looking long term and you're trying to play stocks—somebody once told me that if news comes out on a stock and it's been beaten down and beaten down and news keeps coming out on the stock, it's finally to the point where it doesn't really react to the news. That's a lot of times the bottom. The same thing is true on the upside of a stock. If you're playing a stock that has good news, and it keeps going up and up and they keep pumping out news on the stock, and there's news every day, the fact of the matter is that when it stops reacting to that news positively and people start selling it, then that's usually the top. In a lot of cases it's the top. So it's really difficult, like I said, to analyze the news. I think you've got to pay attention to how the stock reacts to the news. I would never trade on news. I don't trade a stock just because of the news that came out. The news is often news that came out overnight. You're listening to yesterday's news every morning. It's rare that news comes out during the day. And if it comes out overnight, then there's really nothing you can do about it except react to it the next day.

Q: How important are charts and graphs?

A: It's nice to know where a stock comes from. It's nice to look at where the stock is compared with where it was during the course of the year. I'll look at the charts to get a bigger perspective. But this kind of perspective isn't what is going to help a trader, who is really focusing on relative highs and lows and not absolute ones. Of course, if you look at a chart and see that a stock has hit a rung, that it's just cracked a 52-week high, you know that you're either looking at something new or something that is about to go back down.

Q: How important are reactions to actions taken by the Federal Reserve? Should traders be using this information?

A: The reactions to meetings of the Federal Reserve often affect the market in unpredictable ways. The most important thing, as always, is to have a plan. If reactions to the Fed go one way, you need to be prepared to handle what will happen next. I would never go in loaded when Greenspan's speaking because in more than a few stocks you're going to lose your ability to get out, to get in and out quickly, if Greenspan doesn't say what you want or if the market reacts differently. So what happens is you're at the mercy of the stock. If the stock's going up, you're in great shape. If it's going down, you're done. There's no way to get out.

Q: Do you think trading in a sense boils down a lot to understanding general market sentiment?

A: No.

Q: How important is it to understand general market sentiment?

A: Here's the problem with general market sentiment, and this is what I've been laughing at CNBC about all day. These guys are sitting there, the market is down 500 points in 3 days or whatever, and oh, it's terrible. There's this and this. They're not predicting anything. They're reacting to it. And in a lot of cases it's nice to kind of think a little bit contrary and then say when everybody starts thinking it's nasty, when everybody is down on it, that's when it's a buy. But like I said, I trade what's on my screen. And I think if you're going to trade in TradeScape Pro or on the first level or whatever, you can't do everything at once. You can't do everything.

Q: When you analyze a stock, what are the different methods of analysis you use? Is it a combination of technical and fundamental analysis?

A: I hear people talk about technical and fundamental analysis, and half of what I've learned is made up on my own, although there are probably real names for what I do—not to belittle what I do, because it's very real. But I wasn't taught Ballinger bands and linear regression charts and all of those other fancy names, but rather I picked up things as I went along. I'm doing that analysis whether I know it or not, although I do not know the formal names for it. What sorts of things do I find helpful? Some of it you can't put into words. It's like going back to the woman at that seminar who got angry. "What are the secrets?" There are no secrets. We're not keeping anything from you; it's just that we do a second-by-second reevaluation of what we're looking at.

For instance, I've been trading the stock Kinexa (CNXT). I've had a feeling since this stock was in the 60s that it was going to a

100 or 150. Now, I probably would have made more money if I just took all my money and put it into it. But for some reason I can't seem to stay on the stock, and on some of its best upruns, I've been flat. But part of it is because I know that it takes some volatile downruns. And I trade it as I see it. That's what being a day trader is. So to anyone coming from a fundamental background who wants to be a day trader, I'd say to take everything you know and throw it out the window and start over. If you're going to be a fundamental trader, you can look at the graphs and you can make your buys and sells sitting at home. But that's not day trading. That's not active trading.

But another thing is spreads. Underlying spreads, resting spreads, trading spreads, bid strength, and offer strength. A lot of times the offer's just 100 shares, and then there might be no stock for another point. So I'm not going to sit there and say I'm going to buy this thing because I might get that 100 shares, but . . . I don't really want 100 shares anyway. But the point is, to get like 1000 shares, you'd have to pay 2 points. So the spread is in reality, it might look like only a half a point, but it's really a point and a half. So you've got to analyze the underlying, where you're going to be able to get in and out. Same thing on the bid. It might look like the bid's strong because there's three market makers, but if they're only there for 100 shares each, in reality, where are you really sure you can get out? But I look at spreads, I look at them tightening, and I watch the market, the way the market's moving a lot of the time.

Q: What's on your mind as you are making a trade?

A: One good trader once said to me you should always be thinking about your plan. That's it. You always want to have a plan. If the stock doesn't do what you thought, you have to have your plan ready to say, "Hold on, it's time to get out now."

I'm basically thinking what's my plan. My plan once I buy something is what am I going to do if this thing goes down, and if it goes up, where am I going to buy more? That's what I was talking about as far as a high-probability situation. If a stock starts doing exactly what you think it's going to do and you bought one already, then you're looking to buy another one if you still think it's a good buy. I'm incorporating spreads, speed, risk, everything right in there as well as the market.

Q: When you were getting into this, how did you get over that intimidation factor of everything from experienced traders to looking at what was on a screen and not knowing half of what was on it? Because what I hear from you is that there is so much information out there and there are so many jazzy names for different ways of using analysis that it is almost better to get your own strategy with which you are comfortable.

A: One thing I always repeat to people I train is to try a lot of different things and learn from the person training you—learn how he or she makes money. But, for the most part, you've got to find what works for you and stick with it—and be willing to change and bend and grow. If that means you only go long on stocks because that is what you are comfortable with, then stick with it. There are people who make their money because they're right one in five times, but when they're right, they have 5000 shares, and they go for a home run. They may make a lot of trades, and when they're wrong, they get out quickly for as little a loss as possible. This is not the ideal strategy for most conservative direct access traders. I go into almost everything looking to make a little bit of money on every trade. That's my strategy, because I basically hate taking losses. But there are some people who take losses better than I do, who'll take the $2000 loss to see if it becomes a $5000 gain. I won't take the $2000 loss, but that's why I also have been doing this successfully for quite some time.

Q: When you train someone to get started in direct access trading, how do you get him or her started?

A: Right off the bat, I put them on a training module, and I get them to learn the keys—the keys as in terms of how to buy, how to sell, and how to do executions on ECNs. I also make sure they understand about the different ECNs and what they should be looking at on each, such as the bids, offers, spreads, last prints, and volumes. They've got to demonstrate that they know these things like the back of their hand before they ever do a single live trade. Then when they do their first live trade, it's going to be for 100 shares. No more. And it's probably going to be a basic buy in on an offer, look to sell it on an ECN—as it's going up. And if it doesn't do that, they probably sell it as quickly as possible to mitigate their loss.

They basically just need to get used to seeing how stocks move. Different stocks move different ways, and it's just a gaining experience type of thing. The goal is really not to make money in the beginning but not to lose money. The key is to just really gain some experience. The more hours you log sitting in front of a computer watching stocks, the better you're going to get. Once you get into it, then it's just trying different things, but always remember to limit your downside. The other thing to really keep in mind is spreads in the beginning. I don't recommend getting involved in anything more than a quarter-point spread. And it's hard, but stay away from the Microsofts, Dells, and Ciscos because they trade in sixteenths. They become easy targets for a new trader, but it is much easier to get faked out because often they move with no real rhyme or reason. I mean, they move for very good reasons when they make their moves. But if I'm taking on a position in Microsoft, I'm probably doing a trade more along the lines of buying 1000 shares and holding them for 3 points. Because within a quarter or half point, I've got no idea where it's going. I'm just going to continue to lose eighths and quarters on it if I'm going to try to trade that stock that way, but there are other stocks that I can make eighths and quarters on all day long.

Q: What are the typical mistakes that you see new direct access traders making most frequently?

A: I talked to you before about stocks trading in a range, and I think a very typical mistake is when a lot of beginning traders find a stock that has that quarter-point spread, but it's trading in a ⅜ range. So what happens is it's kind of called the ⅜ game—where they're buying it because they see a high-bid lift offer, and then they're paying the offer. The stock is not going anywhere, and what's really happening is the stock is trading in a ⅜ range, but they don't see it. Not seeing the range is big. That's the other thing that I tend not to do, and that I don't like anyone I'm training to do, is never just punch up a stock and buy it. You punch up a stock and you watch it, and then you decide when to buy it so that you do not fall into the range game. Basically, what often happens is that they take the same stock and they play it over and over and over. They buy it at the same price and sell it at the same price because they don't realize that they're in a range. They are actually losing ⅛ and ¼ or ⅜ and ½ every time they do it. They don't realize that it's not breaking out of that range. I fell victim to it for a long time until I realized that stocks trade in ranges. You've got to recognize the range so that you can buy at the bottom and sell at the top of the range. Then, when it breaks out of that range, it's probably going to go somewhat significantly beyond. Now basically all I'm looking at is the range, and I know that it's probably going to make a significant move when it breaks out. So when it breaks out, I buy as much as I can and hold it for a second to see if it actually makes its run. And if it doesn't, I sell it right away. Sometimes it pauses, and it actually goes up, but I'm not going to open myself up to a lot of risk, and that's why I'll make the sale. My trading style, however, depends on recognizing the range that stocks are in.

Q: What gives you confidence as a trader?

A: Experience. That's all it is. Day after day doing it over and over. I've seen new person after new person who comes in doing this, who after 3 months, 6 months, 9 months, a year—somewhere along the line—a light bulb goes on in their head. You can literally see it happen, and all of a sudden, they feel like they know what they're doing. No matter how big a loss someone takes, there's a level of confidence that's like "Hey, I know how to trade. I know how to make money. I may have just done something really stupid that could have been avoided, but I know how to make money." So that's the confidence, and once you make some consistent money over time, you get a lot more comfortable with everything.

Q: For new direct access traders who want to become day traders and make this their profession, it sounds like the key is really just trying to be positive on a daily basis.

A: Yes, and that's why I say just set a first goal of just being positive. Then shoot for $500 a day, then $1000, and so forth, but take your time. Just because you may go out one day and do extremely well with it and hit a new goal does not mean that it is time to move on. You need to do it for at least a month consistently. And this takes a lot of time. I mean, the time that it might take to go from positive to $500 to $1000 to $2000 could be 6 months. You have got to realize this and give it the space and the time to learn. Doing this is a great source of confidence. Saying I know how to make $1000 a day and now I'm going to learn how to make $2000 a day is a very good feeling. And to do this it often means you start expanding your borders such as trading more, getting involved in different stocks, or buying more shares of the same stocks. It's doing the same thing you know, but kind of pushing it up a level. And if that's not working, well you have the confidence to go back and do what you were doing before.

Q: For somebody who is just getting into it, what should their expectations be, realistically?

A: I think anybody who's planning on doing this with any sort of money that they can't risk is just crazy. If you're sitting there in the craziest stocks at home trying to play on TradeScape Pro or E*TRADE or anything like that, you're competing against guys with direct access who are superfast typists—all kids who went to good colleges, very solid colleges. And in most cases these guys don't care, because they don't have a family, don't have anybody to feed if they lose a little bit of money. They're not going to jump out of a window, but they are willing to take more risks. Very risk tolerant. If you're going to compete against those people, it better be with risk money that you can afford to lose.

Q: So how should people who are just starting out compensate for this?

A: At the beginning you want to stay in slower-moving stocks—relatively slower ones. If it's not moving, you don't play it. But my new trainees—I won't let them play IPOs. They are probably the fastest moving stocks out of everything. I won't let them play any stocks really on the news or something that's flying one way or the other because they're going to lose money. And I say this to them: I usually let them do it once, and then I show them. Ha, ha, I told you. The reason you got smoked is because you're playing against Joe Trader who's the fastest typist in the room. You can forget about getting him out of the stock. So I say find something a little bit slower moving, still with volume. Dell can have volume, but it sometimes doesn't move more than a point all day. So something with a few-point range or whatever.

Q: What do you find are some of the weird things that people would not necessarily think they have to be good at, such as typing, for example?

A: Typing, reading spreads. What the real spread is as far as getting in and out. Not just the bid and the offer. That's what the spread looks like. That's the problem. If you're looking at E*TRADE, you're looking at 100 shares in the offer, 100 shares on the bid. Where are you going to get in and out if you've got to play 1000 shares? So it all depends on the size. But even if it says 100 shares, you can assume you're not going to get the bid or the offer, even on E*TRADE or TradeScape Pro or whatever. So I think that speed is extremely important, and you always, always, always have to have a plan. It's one of the most important things. Even if you're stuck in something and you just got smoked, come up with a new plan, even if it's some ridiculous plan, even if Goldman Sachs drops, I'm going to hit the bid now. I've just lost $1 in the stock. I've just lost a point. I don't want to hit the bids because I've lost so much money already. Well if the stock makes another down move at this point, you want to get out because you can probably get it back cheaper, even if you think it's going to go back up later or it's never going to go back up, and there's no more money backing that. So you've got to set a plan all the time and attempt to stick to it. Always readjust your plan.

If something changes, readjust to that. If Goldman Sachs flips. If he's the buyer, and you're saying I'm going to buy until this Instinet drops the bid. Goldman Sachs is on the bid with the Instinet, that's fine, but if all of a sudden Goldman Sachs flips and he's the man, now the situation is different, and now you're going to say I'm going to take that Instinet and use that as my opportunity to get out. Goldman Sachs is an important player in the stock also. So your new plan just readjusted because Goldman Sachs flipped the offer, so I'm making a trade on Instinet.

Q: What do you consider to be the pluses and minuses of trading for a living?

A: There are obvious pluses in that it can be very lucrative, but more important, I love being my own boss. I can't think of anything better. I'm able to make a lot of money, and I don't really have to answer to anyone. It's just me. I've got no one else to blame. I've got no one to rely on. It's just me doing my own thing, and it's up to me to do it, so nobody lets me down but me.

Q: What about the negatives that people should be aware of? One of the things I have inferred from you is that you need to be there day in and day out, and just because you are your own boss does not mean you can take off every Friday.

A: I can tell you that if you don't want to be there day in and day out, it's probably not for you. That's what I meant when I spoke about the love for the markets you need to have. For example, yesterday I was sick, and while I was watching CNBC from home, I kept thinking to myself how much I wish I could be trading. I might have lost money yesterday, who knows, but it doesn't really matter. I wanted to be there, and that's the important part. Not that every day I love doing this. Sometimes it does become tedious and frustrating, especially if I am losing money. But the fact of the matter is that I love it overall, and you have to love it or you're probably not going to succeed at it.

Q: What is it that you love about it?

A: It's the action and the lure of money. It's exactly why so many people are fascinated with Wall Street in general. It's exciting. You have a front-row seat on Wall Street. Having the ability to get involved and watch stocks move up and down as you try and calculate their next movements is really amazing. What is it that I love about it? It's exciting.

Q: How important is it to actually love it?

A: I think it's extremely important only because it's very obsessing. You obsess about it all the time at night if you're doing it full time. I don't know about everybody, but if you're doing it in this office, and I really think you're probably going to drive yourself nuts if you're thinking about something that you don't like all the time. That's my personal opinion. I would never tell anybody to do this just for the sake of money. They've really got to enjoy the thrill of it. Anybody can enjoy something when they're making money.

Q: When you started, you used to hear so much about the edge people had when they worked at Goldman Sachs or Merrill Lynch. Can you compete with them more now than you could before?

A: Obviously, someone at Goldman Sachs who is trading is trading off of order flows has a large advantage in terms of knowing what they need to know to help their customers. But it's the customers who really have the disadvantage, and that's where I have the advantage. I'm trading for myself, and I'm trading right up there with Morgan Stanley or Merrill Lynch. I have the same access to the same market that they do. It used to be when I first started, Instinet was separate, and we did not have access to Instinet. So I didn't even know there was another whole quote that Instinet was trading that was doing half the volume of the shares that were moving through the markets. Now, with Instinet going directly onto Nasdaq, when that order comes through, I have access to it—I can buy or sell depending on what I see. My advantage is that I don't have to pay a "middleman."

Q: What do you think will happen if we do see a market crash?

A: Well, the Dow was down over 200 points at some point today, and the Nasdaq was down 60 or 70, so I basically sold all my positions and sat back and waited. I think that we have the best advantage in the market in that respect because I can get out of my positions quicker than 99 percent of the people with money in the markets. I've got instant access to the market and can exit positions instantly if I so choose. Individuals who aren't watching their stocks on a daily basis are obviously going to get hurt much more in a crash. Especially if they are not using direct access trading tools, they could really get stuck holding the bag. However, long term, I think the markets are going to continue to be positive.

Q: What are the trading rules you live by in terms of taking a conservative approach to direct access trading?

A: The most important thing I try to do is not get emotional. I also make sure to set a high risk to reward level, in terms of not risking a lot but having the opportunity to make a lot. What I do is basically establish a 3:1 risk to reward or better. This means that I'll risk a third of whatever I'm looking to make or better. I never like to put $1000 on the line to make $1000. If I'm buying 1000 shares of a

stock with a very thin bid and a small point spread, I better be
looking for the thing to go up a lot. Otherwise, I'm just going to
buy 100 shares. Basically, I go into every trade thinking I'm going
to make three times as much as I'm risking. I am also very wary of
the risk I am opening myself up to on any given stock. Some stocks
are obviously more volatile than others, and you have to know what
you are getting yourself into. Knowing your risk at all times is
important in every stock you trade. Also, it is always critical to have
a plan. Don't just buy to buy or sell to sell.

Q: What do you think the future holds for direct access traders? Do
you think that someday everyone is going to have direct access to
the markets on some level?

A: Everybody always wants to buy things at the best price. The only
way they can do this is using direct access. Therefore, I think that
the markets are naturally heading that way. I also think it would be
criminal for the Securities and Exchange Commission (SEC) or the
National Association of Securities Dealers (NASD) to ever take this
away from people who want it. It should be a fundamental right to
have access to the market like this, and whether people lose money
or not should be irrelevant if they are told of the risk. Besides, plenty
of ventures have risks; 90 percent of people who go into a casino
lose money, 75 percent of people who open restaurants lose money,
and 50 percent of small businesses fail. Are these people told about
the risks they face before they undertake them? They're not in-
structed about risk. Day traders are told about risk, and they should
be. Loss happens at a quicker pace, but that is what it's all about. I
can't see direct access ever going away, and as long as there's direct
access and as long as there's a market, there'll be people doing this
and doing this successfully.

Q: It sounds like if you want to be an active trader, it is a full-time
commitment. Would you agree?

A: Yes, but that is not to say you that you will not have time for other
things. Going back to the pros versus the cons, it is very intense
during trading hours, but it's not that time-consuming. So the time
that I put in, I try to put in 110 percent. But it doesn't take 110
percent of my time. Trading can only happen from 9:00 A.M. to

4:30 P.M. Monday through Friday. It's necessary to do some outside work, but I have time to do other things. If I wanted to do real estate on the weekends or run a small business on the weekends, I could do it.

Q: But during trading hours, is it always absolutely necessary to be trading, to be watching the market?

A: There are times that it slows. But unless you've logged a ton of experience hours, you can't just turn on the computer, start trading, and an hour later turn it off. It's easy to get hurt this way. I know people who can do this, but it's because they put in their 2 years of 8 to 5 and 110 percent every minute they were there. Now, they haven't seen it all, but they've seen a good 85 percent of it. And so they know what a stock's doing just by looking at it. But that comes with experience. You can't do it part time to learn it.

Q: What sorts of new opportunities do you think will emerge?

A: I think that there have been people who have been somewhat addicted to options who will really start to take advantage of direct access to trade them. Options are just the tip of the iceberg in terms of what will emerge, but the key is just to find what you are comfortable with and stick to it. Don't get lured by other things, especially if you don't know what you are doing. Find what works for you, and stick with it. If it's not working, but you still love the markets, maybe you'll want to start trading the Nikkei when it becomes technologically available to us, or maybe you just want to trade in the middle of the night. The opportunities are endless. Personally, I'll probably never deviate from the Nasdaq unless it's not working for me because it's what I know. I spend so much time watching the Nasdaq and learning and trying to evolve with it as it changes that I couldn't begin to take on another market.

Q: So learning another one of these opportunities would be like starting all over again?

A: It would be, but I do think other opportunities are going to come up, and those who learn them first will be rewarded very well. With respect to day trading, individuals will definitely start day trading additional types of investment vehicles on exchanges all over the world as soon as they can.

WORKSHEETS

Worksheets are an important tool for every direct access trader. Only by learning from both your successes and your failures can you become a better trader. This means analyzing winning and losing trades at the end of trading days, on a quarterly basis, and/or on an annual basis, to examine what you thought was happening in a stock and what actually happened, and mapping out the information that is going to be important to watch over the course of the next trading day. In addition, by working through things such as your profit and loss statement, risk profile, and capital diversification sheets, you can increase your chances for success exponentially. Direct access trading provides you with more tools than ever before. However, this also means that you must learn how to use them and then monitor the results on a frequent basis to find out what is working and what is not. In addition, by clearly mapping out your financial goals, you are giving yourself a clear set of guidelines to look at when developing your trading strategy. Every type of direct access trader needs to take the time to do these worksheets. Remember that the markets are always changing, and therefore, the rules of the game are changing as well. These worksheets will help you in identifying when this is happening and the changes you need to make to adapt and thrive. Sometimes you do not even realize certain trends are happening until you write them down on paper. This appendix will show you a number of worksheets for different types of direct access traders.

DAY TRADER

Amount of risk capital

Goals

	Financial	Strategy
Month 1		
Month 2		
Month 3		
Month 4		
Month 5		
Month 6		

Amount of risk capital for day trading
Amount of capital for investing

Goals

	Financial	**Strategy**
Month 1		
Day trading		
Investing		
Month 2		
Day trading		
Investing		
Month 3		
Day trading		
Investing		
Month 4		
Day trading		
Investing		
Month 5		
Day trading		
Investing		
Month 6		
Day trading		
Investing		

Amount of capital for investing

Goals

	Financial	**Strategy**
Month 1		
Month 2		
Month 3		
Month 4		
Month 5		
Month 6		

REAL-TIME NEWS AND INDICATORS

Selected sources of indicators   **Source**   **News and indicators hit list**

General news sites
Chat rooms and message boards
CNBC

Target news list

Fed announcements
Inflation reports
Analyst reports
Lawsuits
Acquisitions
Hires and fires
Key partnerships
Similar IPOs
War
Institution announcements
Long bond

WHAT TYPE OF TRADER AM I?

Trader characteristics

Personal financial goals

3 Months

6 Months

1 Year

5 Years

20 Years

Risk comfort level

Aggressive
Moderate
Conservative

Risk capital available
Investment capital available
Other

Notes:

PROFIT AND LOSS STATEMENT: DAILY (FOR DAY TRADERS)

Stocks traded	Profit/loss	Explanation	Points to remember

Total stocks traded
Total profit/loss

Overall comments on the trading day:

Points to remember about announcements affecting my stocks today:

Stocks to trade tomorrow:

Stocks to remove from trading list:

PROFIT AND LOSS STATEMENT: MONTHLY

Stocks traded	Profit/loss	Explanation	Points to remember

Total stocks traded
Total profit/loss

Overall comments on the trading month:

Points to remember about announcements affecting my stocks:

Stocks to buy/sell for my portfolio:

PROFIT AND LOSS STATEMENT: QUARTERLY

Stocks traded	Profit/loss	Explanation	Points to remember

Total stocks traded
Total profit/loss

Overall comments on the trading quarter:

Points to remember about announcements affecting my stocks:

Stocks to buy/sell for my portfolio:

KEYBOARD NOTES

Function   **Key stroke**

Buy

Sell

Pull up news

Pull up quote

Plot chart

Check breaking news

Other

Other

Other

Other

TARGET STOCKS

Internet industry

_____

Technology industry

_____

Biotechnology industry

_____

Blue chips

_____

Other

_____

Other

_____

BIBLIOGRAPHY

Aspatore, Jonathan. *Fire Your Broker and Trade Online.* New York: McGraw-Hill, 2000.

Baird, Bob, and Craig McBurney. *Electronic Day Trading to Win.* New York: Wiley, 2000.

Farrell, Christopher. *Day Trade Online.* New York: Wiley, 2000.

Friedfertig, Marc, and George West. *The Electronic Day Trader.* New York: McGraw-Hill, 1998.

Gonzales, Fernando, and William Rhee. *Strategies for the Online Day Trader.* New York: McGraw-Hill, 1999.

Harris, Sunny. *Electronic Day Trading 101.* New York: Wiley, 2000.

Nassar, David. *How to Get Started in Electronic Day Trading.* New York: McGraw-Hill, 1999.

Smith, Gary. *How I Trade for a Living.* New York: Wiley, 2000.

INDEX

ABOUT THE AUTHORS

Jonathan Aspatore is the founder of EPS Business Partners, which provides entrepreneurial solutions to companies worldwide. The author of numerous books, including *The New Electronic Traders* and *Fire Your Broker and Trade Online.* Aspatore is a monthly columnist for a number of Web sites and publications.

Dan Bress is a graduate of Harvard University, and has conducted extensive market research on the direct access industry. His primary area of focus is the technological and financial implication of online trading firms.